P9-DHA-469

Le 41.5973
MAR

FINDING

Betty Crocker

The Secret Life of America's First Lady of Food

Susan Marks

Simon & Schuster   New York   London   Toronto   Sydney

SIMON & SCHUSTER
Rockefeller Center
1230 Avenue of the Americas
New York, NY 10020

Copyright © 2005 by Susan Marks
All rights reserved,
including the right of reproduction
in whole or in part in any form.

SIMON & SCHUSTER and colophon
are registered trademarks of Simon & Schuster, Inc.

For information regarding special discounts for bulk purchases,
please contact Simon & Schuster Special Sales at 1-800-456-6798
or business@simonandschuster.com

Designed by Jeanette Olender

Manufactured in the United States of America

1   3   5   7   9   10   8   6   4   2

Library of Congress Cataloging-in-Publication Data
Marks, Susan.
Finding Betty Crocker : the secret life of America's first lady of food /
Susan Marks.
p.   cm.
1. Crocker, Betty—Biography.   2. Cookery.   I. Title.
TX649.C76M37   2005
641.5973—dc22
2004061566

ISBN 0-7432-6501-7

For my dear Mrs. Springer and her daughter

Contents

Finding Betty Crocker

Introduction

The day before the Fourth of July, I stopped by my parents' house and was not surprised to find my mother busy in the kitchen, baking a red-, white-, and blue-layered cake from Betty Crocker mixes.

"Do you remember when I thought you were Betty Crocker?" I asked.

My mother smiled. "I sure do."

"You were about seven," she recalled, "and it was your turn to bring the treat bucket to your Brownie troop meeting. Instead of buying something, I thought it would be fun to bake cookies together. So I found a chocolate chip cookie recipe from my files called 'Betty Crocker's Bisquickies.' "

"You seemed delighted, so I suggested we bake another batch sometime," my mother explained. "Then you stood right here at the kitchen counter and started flipping through my Betty Crocker cookbook and became convinced that Betty's picture was actually me."

While my mother and I baked the Bisquickies, she shared her childhood memories of an ongoing debate about Betty Crocker. Was she a real person? Household opinion was deeply divided. In the spring of 1950, my grandma wrote to Betty Crocker for

  1

some advice on meal planning and received a reply in return. But, she wondered, was the letter signed "Cordially yours" truly from "Betty" herself?

Absolutely, thought my mother, because Betty had her own radio show and cake mixes. Years later, a women's magazine called Betty "an ageless thirty-two." As a kid, my mother's powers of reason were wholeheartedly straightforward. In her mind, "ageless" was proof that Betty Crocker had an age, just as any real woman did. But my grandmother still wasn't so sure.

Fast-forward to 1998: my grandmother was visiting from out of town. She was thrilled to hear that I was writing a book on Betty Crocker and promised to bring Betty Crocker recipe booklets on her next visit. As we sat and talked, memories came flooding back. For years, she saved Betty Crocker coupon "points" to help my mom fill her hope chest with Betty's Oneida "My Rose" silver pattern. I was surprised to hear my grandmother speak of how controversial cake mixes such as Betty's were when they first came on the market.

With her next visit came an unexpected surprise. Standing in my parents' kitchen, my grandmother handed me something she had cherished since 1950. It was that letter from Betty Crocker. For the first time in my life, I was speechless.

I never imagined that this little piece of history would survive all these years. So much of culinary history is steeped in an oral tradition—mothers teaching daughters, who in turn share their stories of kitchen wisdom with daughters of their own. But Betty Crocker had a hand in changing all that. Before cookbooks and recipe files were commonplace, Betty encouraged my grandma, and millions of Americans like her, to write in search of answers, guidance, or friendly advice.

Into this great divide stepped Betty Crocker with her kitchen

Betty Crocker

General Mills, Inc., Home Service Department

Minneapolis 1, Minnesota

May 19, 1950

My dear Mrs. Springer,

It was most kind of you to write and tell me how
much you enjoy using our PARTYCAKE Mix. I was
glad to know it came to the rescue when your
daughter requested some cupcake May baskets. The
little cakes must have looked very pretty with their
colored icing and the ribbon bows.

You will find that the PARTYCAKE Mix, DEVILS FOOD
CAKE Mix and the GINGERCAKE and Cooky Mix are all
grand time savers. Each one makes a delicious cake
which your family and your friends are sure to
enjoy.

The bulletins you asked for are being sent to you
under separate cover. I hope you find our suggestions
helpful in your meal planning.

Cordially yours,

Betty Crocker

inspirational, "You can do it, and I can help you." Empowered by her words, countless women—and men—made a collective connection, not to Betty Crocker the corporate symbol, but to Betty Crocker the person. But who was she, really? *Finding Betty Crocker* chronicles an American search for her identity that stretches over fifty states and across the turn of a century.

"Born" in 1921 in Minneapolis, Minnesota, to proud corporate parents, Betty Crocker has grown, over eight decades, into one of the most successful branding campaigns the world has ever known. In 1945, *Fortune* magazine named her the second most popular American woman, right behind Eleanor Roosevelt, and dubbed Betty America's First Lady of Food. And in 2000, an *Adweek* poll revealed that a majority "voted" for Betty Crocker in a mock presidential contest, beating out a ballot of five other (Mr. Clean, Mr. Goodwrench, Aunt Jemima, Ronald McDonald, and Cap'n Crunch) brand icons.

What is it about Betty that has motivated so many Americans to award her a place in their hearts and minds? The sheer magnitude—and longevity—of her popularity speaks volumes of the need she has fulfilled in countless lives. Millions have traveled to Minneapolis to tour the Betty Crocker Kitchens, hoping to catch a glimpse of this beloved national icon. And more than a few devoted fans left in tears when they discovered it was impossible to meet her.

But to all the people she's helped, instructed, and even inspired, Betty Crocker has heart. And so she lives on. As for her enduring appeal, perhaps this Depression-era radio listener expressed it best, "Your talks, Betty Crocker, have given me hope."

Chapter One

The Making of an American Myth

Slip-Slide Custard Pie

Custard Pie is known as "Nervous" or "Quaking Pie" in New England because it quivers and shakes. We used to call it "Soggy-crust Pie," too, until a unique slip-slide trick was devised. Here's how to do it!

Baked 9″ Pie Shell
4 eggs (or 8 egg yolks)
⅔ cup sugar
½ tsp. salt

¼ tsp. nutmeg
2⅔ cups scalding hot milk
1 tsp. vanilla, if desired

Heat oven to 350°. Beat eggs slightly. Beat in sugar, salt, nutmeg, milk, vanilla. Pour into ungreased 9″ pie pan. Set pie pan in shallow pan of hot water. Bake *30 to 35* min., just until a sliver knife inserted into filling 1″ from edge comes out clean. The center may look a bit soft but will set later. When lukewarm, loosen custard from pan with knife or spatula. Shake gently to loosen completely. Slip custard into cooled baked pie shell. Let settle a few minutes before serving.

From Gold Medal Jubilee, Select Recipes, 1880–1955:
A treasury of favorite recipes modernized by Betty Crocker

Betty Crocker, happy homemaking, and cake mixes are almost synonymous with 1950s American kitchen kitsch, but Betty originally belonged to an entirely different generation. She made her auspicious debut in the roaring twenties thanks to a jigsaw puzzle and the lure of a prize pincushion. The advertising campaign was the brainchild of the Washburn Crosby Company of Minneapolis, Minnesota. Founded in 1877, the company, a forerunner of General Mills, Inc., was the purveyor of Gold Medal Flour. In October 1921, an ad for the brand appeared on the back of the *Saturday Evening Post*, featuring jumbled puzzle pieces—and a premium giveaway. Contestants arranged the cutouts into a small-town main street scene with happy townspeople going about their daily business in view of a prominently displayed sign for Gold Medal Flour.

A pincushion resembling a miniature Gold Medal Flour sack proved an intoxicating lure. Rather unexpectedly, the milling staff found themselves scrambling to honor the 30,000 completed puzzles received by return post. What arrived along with the puzzles was even more surprising: hundreds of letters asking, "How long should I knead dough?," "What's a good recipe for apple pie?," and "Why does my cake fall?"

Normally, Washburn Crosby handled its trickle of consumer mail through its small, in-house advertising department. Under the direction of the department manager, Samuel Gale, the all-male advertising staff would gather professional cooking advice and recipes from the all-female Gold Medal Home Service staff, then forward the information to inquiring customers. However, Gale never felt comfortable signing his own name to such letters;

The puzzle that started it all. This 1921 advertising contest, sponsored by Gold Medal Flour, ran in the *Saturday Evening Post*, generating 30,000 responses, several hundred of which included personal pleas to the Washburn Crosby Company for kitchen guidance.

  10

he lamented that women did not want advice from a *man*, who presumably did not know his way around the kitchen.

Kitchen or no, Gale was facing either a public relations fiasco or the creative opportunity of a lifetime. Envisioning a female chief of correspondence, Gale and his supervisor, James Quint, convinced the company's directors that the Gold Medal Home Service staff was in need of a new member. Neither résumés nor interviews would be required, however, as the perfect applicant was sheer invention.

The first order of business was to choose a name for this fictitious woman. The surname "Crocker" was in honor of William G. Crocker, a recently retired and well-loved director of

the Washburn Crosby Company. And "Betty" sounded cheery, wholesome, and folksy. The pairing produced a simple and unforgettable name that would one day lead the sweet ranks of America's baked-goods royalty—Duncan Hines, Sara Lee, Dolly Madison, and Little Debbie.

To further personalize Betty, Gale held an informal contest among Washburn Crosby's female employees for the most distinctive Betty Crocker signature. The winner was a secretary named Florence Lindeberg, a variation of whose plain but pretty script still adorns all Betty Crocker products. Eager to strengthen customer relations—and to introduce Betty Crocker publicly—Washburn Crosby made it company policy that every single letter regarding recipes, cooking, baking, or domestic advice receive a prompt reply with Betty's signature. Following the puzzle contest, consumer mail steadily increased in volume, making it necessary for Lindeberg to train numerous female employees in the proper way to sign Betty's replies.

The Betty Mystique

No one could have predicted that Betty Crocker's signature would still be appearing into the next century. Yet from the beginning, the general public had every reason to believe that Betty Crocker was real. From the personalized greeting to the closing of "Cordially yours," a letter from Betty Crocker felt like the genuine article. As routine writers to Washburn Crosby discovered, not only was Betty a gracious correspondent who displayed a keen interest in making women's lives a little easier, but her replies could be counted upon to be informative, prompt, and discreet. By sending her suggestions and recipes directly to homemakers, Betty kept their kitchen confessionals completely confidential—safe from the prying eyes of friend, neighbor, or mother-in-law. Like a trusted friend, or even a mother, Betty could be counted upon never to pass judgment, always to give freely of her wisdom and advice.

Betty's usefulness in the kitchen rose in tandem with the twentieth-century electrical and industrial innovations that would forever alter the time-honored traditions of home and hearth. As the historian Susan Strasser has noted, those "big, shiny pieces of equipment" like washing machines and refrigerators "saved labor, but they also made work . . . that tended to isolate women in the home." It was precisely this juxtaposition that made Betty's guidance indispensable to navigating the transition between kitchens past and present.

While Betty became famous for touting the "modern way" to

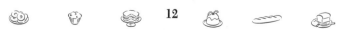

Betty Crocker wasn't Washburn Crosby's only cover girl. The company used a series of ads with maids and housewives to sell flour, including this one for Superlative Flour.

   13

run a kitchen, her philosophy remained deeply grounded in nostalgia. In a reissue of Washburn Crosby's 1910 *Gold Medal Cook Book,* Betty Crocker eulogized those bygone days before she was "born": "The year of 1910 was a time when the cook of the house spent much of her day in the kitchen preparing meals for a large, hungry family. That was the time when she prepared from scratch her own bread, ice cream, soups, sauces . . . even mayonnaise!"

Ask the Expert

While Betty Crocker is a classic, she is not, in fact, an original. A longtime advertising mainstay, "expert" advice was popularized in the late nineteenth century. One notorious purveyor was Lydia Pinkham, who in 1875 chose her own matronly portrait as a means to market her herbal tonic—Lydia E. Pinkham Vegetable Compound—whose "healthful" ingredients happened to include forty-proof alcohol.

Early-twentieth-century admakers capitalized on the popularity of the late-nineteenth-century domestic science movement and the turn-of-the-century home economics movement by elevating influential females, such as the renowned home economist Fannie Farmer, to the position of trusted national experts. The push to feminize product presentation made sense, considering women controlled 80 to 85 percent of consumer spending.

The pages of product-related brochures, newspapers, and popular women's magazines were an open forum for such expert opinion makers, who were hired to endorse domestic products, write product-specific cookbooks, and give advice, blurring the line between paid advertising and honest testimony. "At Miss

In the early 1920s, Washburn Crosby "Home Service" field representatives traversed the nation, demonstrating the many uses for Gold Medal Flour.

  15

Farmer's Famous School of Cookery in Boston," ran one such product placement, "for the regular class and demonstration work of the school, only Royal Baking Powder is used. . . . Only 2¢ worth of Royal makes a large layer cake lusciously light and tender." Home cooks were invited to send away for "the famous Royal Cook Book—over 350 delicious, tested recipes for all kinds of foods."

Upon her debut in 1921, Betty Crocker added her voice to a chorus of female domestic experts—Mary Dale Anthony for S.O.S. scouring pads; Mary Hale Martin for Libby's; and Aunt Sammy (Uncle Sam's wife) for the U.S. Bureau of Home Economics. These and all "personal advisers" were presented as actual women, but only a few were. The distinction seemed of little consequence.

The Flour Wars

The allure of Betty Crocker resided in her practical, thoughtful, and timely messages. Washburn Crosby's Sam Gale cited a busy college lifestyle as the reason young women missed the "apprenticeship of the stove" as traditionally taught by mother and grandmother. To some extent, he was right. The prize was a rich one for a company that could deliver the perfect product, via the perfect representative.

In 1920, the population of the United States was approaching 106 million and a typical family spent hundreds of dollars a year on meat, vegetables, eggs, and flour. Competition for flour dollars was fierce, as Gold Medal, Pillsbury, and others sought to win over Mrs. America and create brand loyalty.

In 1924, Pillsbury Flour Mills—the Minneapolis-based company whose "Family of Foods" included Pillsbury's Best Flour,

Pancake Flour, Buckwheat Pancake Flour, Health Bran, Wheat Cereal, Rye Flour, Graham Flour, and Farina—featured the "Eat More Wheat" slogan created in 1923 by Washburn Crosby. Consumers were invited to "Pour a little Pillsbury's Pancake Flour into your hand. Note the creamy-white color due to Pillsbury's high-grade flours. Rub it with your finger—see how smooth it is—its fine velvety texture."

Inglehart Brothers millers of Evansville, Indiana, also stood by the quality of their Swans Down brand, "twenty-seven times as fine as good bread flour." A 1925 advertising campaign added, "It takes 100 pounds of the finest wheat to make 26 pounds of Swans Down. There's nothing to it but wheat, the choicest to be bought. Not one atom of corn starch or any other ingredient has been added."

For the Aunt Jemima Mills Company (purchased by the Quaker Oats Company in 1925), quantity and quality went hand in hand. A January 1924 advertisement announced: "Over 500 million Aunt Jemima Pancakes were served last year." In March of that same year, readers learned "What Aunt Jemima's Secret Was." Success was in the ingredients: "Aunt Jemima didn't use ordinary flour for her pancakes; she used a special kind, an exceptionally fine grade of wheat flour. And then she mixed with it smaller quantities of other flours seldom found in stores today."

Betty's company's concern for quality made for boldface copy in a 1926 advertising campaign. "Last year we held back more than 5 million pounds of Gold Medal flour. Chemically, it was perfect. But our 'Kitchen-test' proved it varied slightly in the way it acted in the oven. It could not carry the Gold Medal Label." What Gold Medal Flour did carry was an "Unqualified Guarantee." "If it is not the best flour that you have ever tried and if it does not produce the most uniformly good results, you

  17

Now a renowned cooking expert
tells a new way to perfect baking results

Last year alone, 300,000 grateful women wrote Betty Crocker about her "Kitchen-test" of flour and how it has made their baking results more uniform

I am sure that every woman, no matter how wonderful a cook, will be interested in this new discovery in baking. A discovery that eliminates 50% of the cause of baking uncertainties—ends those heart-breaking moments when you want everything to be perfect, only to have a prize recipe turn out a trifle heavy or soggy—sometimes a complete failure.

Recently chemists and cooking experts, working together, found that *flour* is 50% of the cause of baking failures.

They discovered that while chemists' tests might prove two batches of the *same brand* of flour exactly alike chemically, these two batches might act entirely different in your oven—bring fine results in one case and spoil a good recipe another time.

That is why we, some time ago, inaugurated the now famous "Kitchen-test" for Gold Medal Flour. Every time one of our mills turns out a batch of flour, we bake cakes, pastries, biscuits, breads—everything—from this batch according to standard recipes. Unless each batch bakes to standard, the flour is sent back to be re-milled.

This means one flour for all your baking. Over 2,000,000 women now know there is no better flour for cakes and pastries. Why pay more?

Money-Back Guarantee

Last year we re-milled more than five million pounds of Gold Medal Flour. Our chemists reported it perfect, but it didn't act right in our test kitchen ovens.

So, today, every sack of Gold Medal Flour that comes into your home is "Kitchen-tested" before you receive it. The words, "Kitchen-tested" are stamped on the sack.

We guarantee not only that Gold Medal is a light, fine, snow-white flour. We also guarantee that it will always act the same way in your oven. Your money refunded if it doesn't.

Special—for the South

Gold Medal Flour (plain or self-rising) for our Southern trade is milled in the South at our Louisville mill. Every batch is "Kitchen-tested" with Southern recipes before it goes to you.

Special Offer
"Kitchen-tested" Recipes

Recipes we use in testing Gold Medal Flour are rapidly becoming recognized standards. We have printed these "Kitchen-tested" Recipes on cards and filed them in neat wooden boxes. Handy for you in your kitchen.

We will be glad to send you one of the new Gold Medal Home Service Recipe Boxes, complete with recipes, for only $1.00 (less than this service actually costs us). Twice as many recipes as in original box. Just send coupon with check, money order or plain dollar bill. This offer only good if you live in the United States.

If you prefer to see first what the recipes are like, we will be glad to send you selected samples, including Orange Pie—FREE.

Check and mail the coupon for whichever you desire.

Orange Pie. A new favorite. Refreshing and delicate! The result of many tests in the Gold Medal Kitchen. Kitchen-tested recipes with Kitchen-tested Flour—perfect results always.

Pleased! "I have not used Gold Medal Kitchen-tested Flour very long, but I am certainly pleased with the results I am receiving."
Mrs. J. A. McCutcheon,
4005 Chambers St., Milwaukee, Wis.

Confidence! "I am a rooter for Gold Medal Kitchen-tested Flour. It is so convenient to use the same flour for both bread and cakes and know that you will have perfect results."
Mrs. Francis L. Cusdon, Brighton, Mass.

It's a Joy! "With Gold Medal Kitchen-tested Flour results are perfect and I am beginning to feel so sure of having things turn out successfully that baking is a joy."
Mrs. Adda L. Gray,
97 Hancock St., Cambridge, Mass.

Listen for Betty Crocker and her "Kitchen-tested" recipes over your favorite radio station

One view of the Gold Medal Kitchen where every batch of Gold Medal Flour is Kitchen-tested before it gets to you

GOLD MEDAL FLOUR

Kitchen-tested

Washburn Crosby Company, General Offices, Minneapolis

MILLS AT MINNEAPOLIS, BUFFALO, KANSAS CITY, CHICAGO, LOUISVILLE, GREAT FALLS, KALISPELL, OGDEN

Betty Crocker

Send coupon now. A new delight awaits you.
MISS BETTY CROCKER
Gold Medal Flour
Home Service Dept.
Dept. 800   Minneapolis, Minn.
( ) Enclosed find $1.00 for your box of "Kitchen-tested" Recipes. (It is understood that I may, at any time, send for new recipes free.)
( ) Please send me selected samples of "Kitchen-tested" Recipes—FREE.

Name _____
Address _____
City _____ State _____

Gold Medal Flour magazine ad, 1927.

  18

may at any time return the unused portion of your sack of flour to your grocer. He will pay you back your full purchase price. We will repay him."

As competing advertisements in the October 1926 issue of *McCall's* suggest, cost was a kingdom all its own. "Always a bargain at the same price," headlined a Pillsbury promotion. "Often you can buy Pillsbury's Best Flour at a price as low as other flours, in spite of the big difference in quality. . . . It is the enormous output of the giant Pillsbury Mills which makes possible the production of such a high-quality flour at such a moderate price." To which the Gold Medal Flour advertisers replied, under the signature of Betty Crocker, "There is no better flour for cakes and pastries. Why pay more?" Yet neither miller divulged flour prices in their ads.

In fact, Washburn Crosby was willing to pay more—to develop and disseminate the "Kitchen-test" concept that anchored the Gold Medal sales plan. The process was explained to consumers in elaborate, loving detail: "First the Gold Medal millers with their 60 years of experience carefully select the choicest wheat. Before they mill it they wash every grain in clear running water. Then samples of each batch are sent daily to the Gold Medal Kitchen. In this cheerful kitchen, Miss Betty Crocker and her staff bake from these samples." With her first-hand experience, Betty Crocker was just the person to explain how "2,000,000 women have learned to make perfectly delicious small breads and pastries every time they bake."

In April 1926, "Miss Crocker" invited consumers to send 70¢ for a "neat wooden box" filled with "delightful new recipes." By November of that same year, a new and improved offer was available—for just thirty cents more. "We will be glad to send you one of the New Gold Medal Home Service Recipe boxes, com-

  19

plete with recipes, for only $1.00 (less than this service actually costs us). Twice as many recipes as in original box. Just send coupon with check, money order, or plain dollar bill."

The ad copy was signed Betty Crocker, just as all her letters were. And the promotion, like so many more to come, proved to be what Betty's newfound public was looking for. A woman from Randolph, Minnesota, wrote, "Never again will I fool with other flour. With Gold Medal Kitchen-tested Flour my biscuits are wonderful dainties. The cakes also, especially the sponge cake. I'm a Gold Medal booster forever." From Buffalo, New York, came further testimony: "I am always singing Gold Medal Kitchen-tested Flour's praises and I have introduced a number of my friends to use it instead of having two kinds of flour [one for baking cakes, another for general purposes]."

Betty's People

While the immediate response to Betty Crocker's service was favorable, she was not an overnight success. For the first three years of Betty's existence, she was little more than a signature on the bottom of a letter, recipe, or advertisement. Word of her was spread by the company's professional, college-educated home economists. Washburn Crosby, typical of many Progressive-era companies, looked to its Home Service Department to highlight its forward-thinking policies. Operating from a tiny test kitchen at Washburn Crosby headquarters, the early Gold Medal Home Service Department (eventually known as the General Mills Home Service Department and, later, as the Betty Crocker Kitchens) was entrusted with a public relations mission of unprecedented magnitude: the shaping of Betty Crocker's public persona.

Now—
"Kitchen-tested" Recipes
which are rapidly becoming recognized standards

A New Service to the Women of America

As Betty Crocker and her staff of Home Economics Experts "Kitchen-test" samples of Gold Medal "Kitchen-tested" Flour, many new and delightful recipes are constantly created and *tested*.

These recipes are rapidly becoming recognized standards. They are used by women who have a reputation for their excellent and temptingly different dishes.

We now have these recipes printed on cards—filed in neat wooden boxes—and are offering them to the women of America.

The cost of the cards and the box is only $1. (This is actually less than the service costs us.)

So, if you would gain a reputation for yourself as a marvelous cook, simply send $1.00 to Miss Betty Crocker, c/o Gold Medal Flour Home Service Department, Washburn Crosby Company, Minneapolis, Minnesota, and you will receive these "Kitchen-tested" recipes which are now used by thousands of women everywhere.

Betty Crocker

For $1, homemakers could send away for a little wooden box full of Betty Crocker's recipes. From 1926–28, 350,000 Betty loyalists took Washburn Crosby up on their offer.

   21

Home economists Ina Rowe, Agnes White, Ruth Haynes Carpenter, Blanche Ingersoll, Janette Kelley, and Marjorie Child Husted were the "voice" of Betty Crocker in print and in person. In what would become characteristic Betty style, their communications sought to engage as well as instruct. In one how-to booklet called "What Every Woman Should Know About Baking: The New Meaning of Flour—by Betty Crocker," the lesson followed the "heartbreaking" scenario of a cake that turned out a "wee bit flat, or with a faint suggestion of sogginess." Thanks to the high quality of "Kitchen-tested" Gold Medal Flour, the dessert was saved—as was the day.

At Gold Medal Flour Cooking Demonstrations and Betty Crocker Cooking Schools, the home economists presented Betty Crocker's solutions to common domestic woes. The first Minneapolis and St. Paul–area demonstrations proved so popular that the original staff was expanded by twenty in order to reach women's auxiliary groups, church associations, home economics classes, and county fairs throughout the Midwest, East, and South.

Washburn Crosby home economists traveled from town to town, often stopping for weeks at a time to hold community classes. Local newspapers advertised the Gold Medal Flour demonstrations with open invitations to men, women, and children. It was not unusual for auditoriums to fill to capacity, leaving the overflow crowds to stand in the back and line the windows outside.

Sometimes the setup was the best part of the show. Since auditoriums did not come equipped with fully modern kitchens, Betty's staff had to improvise. Entire towns turned out upon occasion to watch the local fire department assist in the transporting of a borrowed electric stove.

   22

The Betty Crocker staff of 1924 comprised college-educated, professional home economists who tested recipes, conducted cooking demonstrations, answered consumer questions, and helped shape the early persona of Betty Crocker.

   23

Often the entire town turned out for a Betty Crocker Cooking School class or demonstration.

In bigger cities, the home service staff found themselves improvising on a different theme. While their primary purpose was to "demonstrate Gold Medal Flour and its superiority over other brands," the staff also taught extended lessons on housekeeping, child care, nutrition, canning, and sewing. In 1922, staffer Mollie Gold traveled to settlement houses on the east side of New York City to "make people happier, healthier and to make their work easier." She even instructed a boys' class in the "art of camp cookery."

Back in Minneapolis, Betty's home staff was fielding hundreds of letters and even phone calls from homemakers despairing over "baking failures." Endeavoring to make the typical kitchen more like a foolproof scientific laboratory, Washburn Crosby home economists singled out irregular-sized baking pans as the culprit, and took up the crusade for national pan standardization. The size and shape of the pan used in cake making as well as the type of batter affected baking temperature. The *Ladies' Home Journal* home economist Mabel Jewett Crosby heralded "Science in Your Oven": "Perfect pie and pastry [are] yours if you take its temperature." But best of all was a product guaranteed to succeed, like Gold Medal Flour, whose "Kitchentest" saved "*you* from costly experimenting when you bake."

In this pioneering spirit, millions of American homemakers were poised on the brink of transition to the modern age. The marketers of the 1920s were up to the challenge, offering every aspect of a newer and better life, priced to sell.

Good-Bye to Yesterday's Kitchen

The goal was to banish yesterday's kitchen in favor of a more gleaming vision, and Betty Crocker knew where to start. Reviewing a collection of Gold Medal recipes published in 1910, Betty found that changing kitchen technology had quickly put them out of date. "Since many of the ingredients and methods no longer fit the times," she instructed home cooks, "do not try to follow the directions given. Instead, if you discover a recipe you'd love to prepare . . . refer to a more current Betty Crocker" recipe.

"Times certainly have changed for the modern homemaker," Betty reflected on the era she called "the good old days." But good could be better, as Betty demonstrated with her innovative test kitchens, among the first to reap the benefits of the string of inventions begun in 1916 with the introduction of the first electric refrigerator (at about $900, the appliance cost more than a new car) and continued with the first all-electric range in 1917.

"Electrical equipment has made housework not only easier, but more interesting," proclaimed the June 1927 issue of *Mc-Call's*. With Betty nodding her approval, the race was on, first to outfit the home with the latest inventions, then to beat the neighbors at their own game. May B. VanArsdale, professor of "Household Art," and Dorothy E. Shank, an instructor in "Foods and Cookery" at Teachers College, Columbia University, chronicled just such a friendly neighborhood rivalry in their June 1926 article "Now Is the Time for Kitchen Adventures."

Their subjects were the "wide-awake homemakers"–cum– "household engineers" who called themselves the "Up-to-Date Kitchen League." Each member reveals in turn which modern kitchen innovation she prizes above all others. Testimony begins with the kitchen thermometer; then the ante is quickly upped. Mrs. Young "feels she is a step in advance of the other members," thanks to her regulated oven, which frees her from the thermometer. Mrs. Blank points out her ingenuity: she cooks with a bake-pot over the one gas burner in her kitchenette. A fourth member calls her fireless cooker her "greatest friend." Finally, triumphantly, "one of the newest members" of the League brings forth her electric mixer.

A modern kitchen called for modern appliances, each with its own set of instructions. As the Westinghouse Electric and Manufacturing Company pointed out in a 1925 campaign, electricity was the key. "Pressing a button—or pushing a plug into a handy convenience outlet—thus should a modern home—with Westinghouse Electrical Appliances—serve its mistress. . . . Right now is a good time to buy."

"Domestic Science Consultant" Sarah Field Splint, for General Electric's Edison Mazda Lamp line, called out kitchen lighting as yet another essential. "The Kitchen is the cheapest room to light properly," she advised. "Good light costs no more than poor light. It's the cheapest maid you can employ." And in an era when "more than ninety-five out of every one hundred homemakers in this country are keeping house without a maid," who could do without? Waffle irons, warming pads, cabinet electric ranges, toasters, and even a Grecian urn percolator set were on offer to fill every available outlet.

But Can She Cook?

Women attending the Gold Medal Flour demonstrations may have missed their apprenticeship of the stove, but in Betty Crocker's world, technology had rendered Mother's kitchen techniques somewhat obsolete. Recipe adaptation proved particularly daunting to homemakers less experienced with modern appliances. For instance, a traditional recipe for drop biscuits that called for ten minutes' baking in a "quick oven"—meaning a very hot wood-burning or coal-burning stove—now needed to be adjusted for equivalent temperature settings on a gas or electric range. As Betty's staff was quick to point out, the trial-and-error method wasted time and money.

With cooking information not widely available—cooks relied mostly on family recipes and limited-distribution cookbooks—the Gold Medal Home Service Department was truly living up to its name. Maria Parloa, the leading home economist with the famous Boston School of Cooking, wrote *Miss Parloa's New Cook Book* distributed, in part, by the Washburn Crosby Company in 1880. The company went on to publish *Washburn Crosby Co.'s New Cook Book* in 1894 and, in 1903, the *Gold Medal Flour Cook Book*. But cookbooks were expensive not only to produce but to keep in print. Even Fannie Farmer had to pay the printing costs of her eventual best-seller, the *Boston Cooking-School Cook Book* (1896), as her publisher, Little, Brown, was not enthusiastic about its prospects.

By the time Washburn Crosby's cooking demonstrations were popular in the early 1920s, the company's cookbooks were out of print, yet demand hadn't slowed for information on basic meal preparation, menu planning, grocery budgeting, and cooking techniques. Desire for new recipes was constant, given "that remorseless demand of the family for three meals a day."

The Home Service Department never had enough printed Gold Medal Flour recipes to hand out, nor could it keep up with the quantities of recipe requests that arrived by mail. Inserting Betty's recipes in sacks of Gold Medal Flour was one stopgap measure. But the variety of recipes wasn't plentiful enough to satisfy customers who wanted more of Betty. In just a few short years, Betty Crocker was well on her way to becoming Washburn Crosby's living dream.

   28

Vox Feminae

Radio was the big break Betty's people were looking for. In 1920, 5,000 American homes had a wireless set. By 1924, radio ownership soared to 2.5 million. In the autumn of that year, Washburn Crosby decided to see how Betty Crocker would fare over the airwaves. Executives authorized the Home Service Department to launch a radio cooking show designed to take the place of the regional demonstrations and cooking school. The financial risk of Betty's show was not insignificant, considering that neither radio nor Betty Crocker was a household staple.

With radio broadcasting still in its nascent stages—airtime scheduling was not yet standardized, and the first nationwide network, the National Broadcasting Company, would not be established until 1926—its commercial value had yet to be fully proven. Nevertheless, Washburn Crosby took a gamble and purchased a faltering Minnesota radio station, WLAG—The Call of the North. Renamed after its corporate benefactor, the "Gold Medal Station" took the call letters WCCO. With its powerful 5,000-watt AM transmitter, WCCO's signal could reach audiences as far flung as California, Illinois, and Tennessee. The investment proved sound: by 1927 more than 6 million radios were in use. With an average listening ratio of five people per set, the potential national market topped out at 30 million. By comparison, for the first six months of 1924, *Ladies' Home Journal* boasted a net paid circulation of 2,412,688—which was over 15 percent more than its nearest competitor, but just a fraction of radio's reach.

America had never known anything like the splendor of broadcast radio. The surreal world of radio fantasy, from comedy shows like *Amos 'n' Andy* to daytime dramas like *The Guiding*

   29

Light, lured Americans to part with their hard-earned wages. A 1925 advertisement for RCA—whose Radiola Regenoflex and Radiola X models sold for about one quarter of the average monthly family income, between $191 and $245, depending on features—explained the magic: "Each thread of sound reaches your room as it was played or sung—in full richness. Speech is clear, voices are *real.* . . . The engineers have kept pace with the broadcasters—have improved reception to meet an ever-widening world of fun."

"Welcome to our circle"

"The radio made Betty," *Fortune* magazine declared in 1945. "It is fair to say that it did for her career in commerce what it did for Franklin D. Roosevelt's in politics." The Washburn Crosby Company helped pioneer the new "Home Service" radio format when on October 2, 1924, Betty Crocker's show debuted as a casual "womanly talk." On that first broadcast, the home economist Blanche Ingersoll introduced herself as Betty Crocker, announcing that she would be dropping in each day for a visit and a chat about cooking and homemaking:

> *Good morning. This is a very happy morning for me because at last I have an opportunity to really talk to you. To those of you who are my friends through correspondences I wish to extend most cordial greetings and good wishes, and to those of you who are making the acquaintance of Betty Crocker for the first time—I bid you welcome to our circle. This hour—10:45 every morning—is yours and I am here to be of service to you.*

  30

Ingersoll loosely patterned Betty's show after a popular Chicago radio program hosted by Mrs. Peterson of the People's Gas Company. Topics ranged from cooking and "female concerns" to housekeeping and time management to husbands and beaux, friends and relatives, and, of course, Gold Medal Flour. Recipe preparations followed techniques favored by home economists, such as the precise care and measurement of ingredients.

Like the U.S. *Department of Agriculture's Housekeeper's Chats* hosted by Aunt Sammy, Betty Crocker's meal preparation advice, serving suggestions, and recipes were imbued with a philosophy reminiscent of turn-of-the-century domestic science. The shows extolled the virtues of a well-balanced, healthy meal and women's obligation to serve it.

Listeners to Betty's first radio broadcast, entitled "Good Food," learned that a woman who produced unsavory meals risked dire consequences. "If you load a man's stomach with soggy boiled cabbage, greasy fried potatoes," Betty cautioned, "can you wonder that he wants to start a fight, or go out and commit a crime? We should be grateful that he does nothing worse than display a lot of temper."

Not always did the role of homemaker come naturally. Betty observed, "Occasionally we find someone who dislikes it very much." But the condition was not permanent, provided the woman in question was willing to adjust her attitude from the "wrong point of view"—that keeping house is "plain drudgery" that she feels "she is above"—to the more positive stance of realizing that "a good cook" has "a real influence" on the happiness of "big Bob and little Junior."

When it came to prescribing exacting domestic standards for the betterment of the family, Betty talked tough, but her delivery was sweet. A homemaker's aspirations could be "as great as woman could have in any occupation," Betty declared. The answers to these and other secrets could be had as easily as tuning in, within WCCO's broadcast radius, over morning coffee or at work around the house.

> *It may be that you are a young housekeeper eager to learn the hows and whys and wherefores of this big job of cooking for your husband. There are many ways in which I can be of service to you, not only through cooking lessons but with suggestions for serving, for planning your housework, for marketing so that you can get the most for your money. Perhaps I can even help you with your weekly washing or tell you how to remove stains from your best tablecloth, or give you some good suggestions for housecleaning.*

Betty undoubtedly offered realistic and timely advice to women in the 1920s, given their limited options for work outside homemaker, wife, and mother. The commercial motive behind each friendly piece of advice was easy to overlook in the pleasure of Betty's company.

The Betty Crocker Service Program

Washburn Crosby supported the radio broadcasts with advertisements in leading women's magazines. Readers were reminded to "Tune in on Gold Medal Radio Station (WCCO—416.4 meters), St. Paul–Minneapolis. Interesting programs daily. Also cooking talks for women every Mon., Wed., Fri. at 10:45 AM, by Betty Crocker, Gold Medal Flour Home Service Dept." By 1925, two distinct radio programs evolved: *The Betty Crocker*

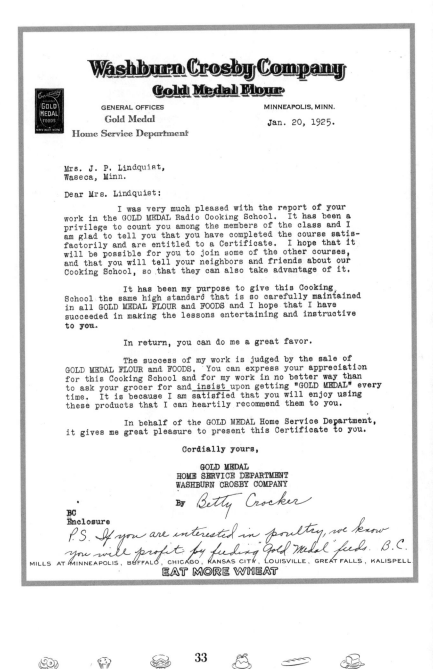

Washburn Crosby Company
Gold Medal Flour

GENERAL OFFICES   MINNEAPOLIS, MINN.

Gold Medal

Jan. 20, 1925.

Home Service Department

Mrs. J. P. Lindquist,
Waseca, Minn.

Dear Mrs. Lindquist:

     I was very much pleased with the report of your work in the GOLD MEDAL Radio Cooking School. It has been a privilege to count you among the members of the class and I am glad to tell you that you have completed the course satisfactorily and are entitled to a Certificate. I hope that it will be possible for you to join some of the other courses, and that you will tell your neighbors and friends about our Cooking School, so that they can also take advantage of it.

     It has been my purpose to give this Cooking School the same high standard that is so carefully maintained in all GOLD MEDAL FLOUR and FOODS and I hope that I have succeeded in making the lessons entertaining and instructive to you.

     In return, you can do me a great favor.

     The success of my work is judged by the sale of GOLD MEDAL FLOUR and FOODS. You can express your appreciation for this Cooking School and for my work in no better way than to ask your grocer for and_insist_upon getting "GOLD MEDAL" every time. It is because I am satisfied that you will enjoy using these products that I can heartily recommend them to you.

     In behalf of the GOLD MEDAL Home Service Department, it gives me great pleasure to present this Certificate to you.

                   Cordially yours,

                   GOLD MEDAL
                   HOME SERVICE DEPARTMENT
                   WASHBURN CROSBY COMPANY

                   By *Betty Crocker*

BC
Enclosure

P. S. If you are interested in poultry, we know you will profit by feeding "Gold Medal" feeds. B. C.

MILLS AT MINNEAPOLIS, BUFFALO, CHICAGO, KANSAS CITY, LOUISVILLE, GREAT FALLS, KALISPELL

EAT MORE WHEAT

In September 1925, what began as Betty Crocker's local radio show on Washburn Crosby's WCCO went national.

Service Program and, on Fridays, *The Betty Crocker Cooking School of the Air* (also called *Gold Medal Flour Radio Cooking School*).

Much to the surprise of many Washburn Crosby executives, thousands of listeners readily participated in Betty's on-air cooking school. The privilege of trying out Betty Crocker's recipes came at no cost to students. Each received a member report questionnaire, to be returned with their completed lessons, along with the grocer's signature, ensuring that students used only Gold Medal Flour. By mailing in the written results of their work, they would qualify to earn their diplomas and graduate in an annual commencement ceremony broadcast. In twenty-seven years of broadcasting, *The Betty Crocker Cooking School of the Air* produced more than a million alumni.

Dear Betty

Brilliantly practical and relevant to listeners' lives, Betty Crocker's radio programs were a hit with her public. Women could not help but express appreciation:

> *With such interesting cooking talks as yours on the radio and available to the majority of housekeepers, I really think it won't be long before we're a nation of inspired cooks.*

> *

> *Please accept my thanks for the recipes and talks. I write each recipe down on a card, as you give them out in such a nice slow way, it makes it easy. In that way, I can make up the recipe very soon if I wish to. So thank you so very much for all the new tricks you've taught me. Forty-five years of cooking and to learn new ways now is wonderful.*

> *

   35

There is just one reason I shall hate to pass on (I'm 77) and that is I'll not get your recipes. However, I shall send in a call to St. Peter, perhaps he'll comply—watch for it. I guess I mean listen.

*

I have listened to every one of your cooking school programs and have decided that I'm not a very good housekeeper. I'm really glad I'm still single.

*

You are certainly a Godsend to young wives (including me) who have recently assumed culinary responsibilities.

*

I can't tell you how very much I enjoy your talks. I wonder if you realize how much you are helping me, or rather I should say "us."

*

The delightful thing about you and your staff is that you make the humdrum exciting.

As Betty noted in an early broadcast, men also took an interest in her cooking shows: "And the men—indeed I have not forgotten the men—I was delighted to have so many of them interested in joining our school." Listeners of both sexes responded dramatically with letters wholly removed from cooking inquiries. Troubles with in-laws, neighborhood quarrels, and disagreeable spouses were just a few of the personal matters listeners asked for Betty's help with. In an era when the quest for improved education and employment routinely drew young women away from their rural roots and into urban centers, Betty often did what Mother was too far away to do—advise, instruct, console.

As the dean of her own cooking school, Betty Crocker ascended from the familiar to the powerful—even mystical—role in American culture that was destined to be hers. No longer one of many home economists offering yet another ringing product endorsement, Betty had become a national authority on food.

National Betty

As listenership grew, so did product loyalty, which in turn drove sales of Gold Medal Flour products. And Betty Crocker's shows contributed greatly to WCCO's success. In 1924, a sample daily playlist allocated two slots for Betty Crocker's "Home Service" segments. And by the end of 1925, Betty Crocker's radio program expanded its broadcast to a total of twelve regional stations. WGR in Buffalo, New York, was the first, followed by stations in New York City, Chicago, Boston, Kansas City, Philadelphia, St. Louis, Pittsburgh, Los Angeles, Cleveland, and Detroit.

At each station, a different woman spoke as Betty Crocker, but all read from the same script, written in the Minneapolis "mother kitchen." In 1925, Bettys around the nation asked, "Won't it be fun to think that you and your sister in Pennsylvania or Ohio and your good friend in Iowa and your aunt in California can all join the same cooking school and have your radio lessons together?"

Betty's cooking show was a national sensation, with 47,000 new registrants. Women and men of all ages, married couples and children were among the students. Blind and housebound students also informed Betty Crocker that her on-air classes were helpful. Welcoming the 1926 graduating class, Betty marveled at the advancing technology of radio:

*Good morning, everybody! I wonder if you realize that we
are making history this morning? This program marks a
new era in the history of broadcasting. Thousands of you,
sitting in your own homes in forty-five states of the United
States, are graduating together as you have gone to school
together, over the air. In this age of wonderful inventions,
such unusual experiences come to us each day that we accept as a matter of course many occurrences that a few
years ago would have been considered miraculous.*

*Our program this morning has never been duplicated. It
would not have been possible twelve short months ago. Our
class is without doubt the largest cooking class that has
ever been organized. It covers the largest territory, has the
greatest number of graduates, and has only one teacher.*

Each week, "tens of thousands" of new letters to Betty arrived,
requesting general cooking and baking tips, as well as advanced
tutoring. Newlyweds in particular felt at a disadvantage in the
modern kitchen: "I am a young bride wanting so much to do
things right in cooking, but so often I make a grand mess of
things. Why don't schools everywhere stress cooking and sewing
more? I could have used that much more than my knowledge of
Latin and Spanish." Continually, homemakers expressed interest
in learning fail-safe baking techniques, new recipes, and quick-
and-easy dishes. In the name of Betty Crocker, every single letter was carefully answered.

The Secret Life of Betty Crocker

Knowledge of Betty Crocker's identity was restricted to company insiders. Brand loyalty was a lucrative proposition, and

Washburn Crosby had much to gain by keeping Betty's secret. From her very first radio broadcast, the truth was carefully guarded, especially by the actresses who played her. The only admission made on air was that Betty Crocker did not do the recipe testing alone, but rather in the company of her growing Home Service staff. It's reasonable to speculate that most listeners genuinely believed in Betty Crocker. Some had an idea that she was based in Minneapolis, and that other women spoke for her on radio stations located in other cities.

No grand conspiracy cloaked Betty Crocker, nor did the milling company deliberately set out to deceive customers. Yet Washburn Crosby did not officially set the record straight for many years. Why risk unnecessarily disappointing Betty's fans at a time when the relationship was still new, untested?

Who's in the Kitchen with Betty?

As the medium of radio matured, so did the *Betty Crocker Service Program* and *Cooking School of the Air*. In the show's fourth season, in 1927, Betty debuted a new style decidedly smoother and more intimate than in previous broadcasts. Marjorie Child Husted, newly promoted from the ranks of Gold Medal Flour home economists to director of the Home Service Department, was responsible for putting the polish on Betty's updated style. Husted's impressive tenure as the woman behind the woman would run for twenty years.

One of her first duties was to take over scripting—and sometimes broadcasting—Betty's radio program. On October 5, 1927, Husted embraced the "diversity" of her audience and expounded on the value of radio:

Marjorie Child Husted, the woman behind Betty Crocker for twenty years. To many, she was Betty Crocker.

I like to picture you as I talk. I can see experienced house-keepers peeling potatoes, or doing some other "sitting down" job while they listen for the little hints which help relieve the monotony of the old routine. I see busy mothers of small children, grandmothers, brides and young house-keepers, and the shut-ins, who are bed-fast or helpless, who tell me they never fail to watch for this hour. . . . Isn't it wonderful that no matter where you are we can meet this way to discuss the things we are all interested in? The radio admits no barrier of time or distance. Not so many years ago we had to go out visiting with near neighbors, perhaps gossiping over the back fence, or we waited for a club meeting or sewing circle to exchange recipes. But now, though I am miles away, I can talk to you, and radio friends in Massachusetts can exchange ideas with those in California.

Marjorie Child Husted was not exactly Betty personified. A graduate of the University of Minnesota who had put in four years with Washburn Crosby, Husted was a woman who knew how to take command, speak her mind, list her numerous achievements, and lecture businessmen on the right way to sell to Mrs. Consumer. A veteran of Red Cross welfare relief work, Husted also had heart. Her relief work took her into poor communities, where women had very few resources. She parlayed her education and experience into a career that tapped into the needs, desires, and burdens of homemakers. Husted's talent for serving the public while turning a corporate profit impressed her supervisors, especially Sam Gale.

Under Husted's direction, Betty Crocker's cooking shows were added to the National Broadcasting Company (NBC) 1927 national lineup. Her show expanded from twenty minutes to one hour, three times a week. Among the first of its kind, as well as the longest-running, *The Betty Crocker Cooking School of the Air* received the highest ratings in its category.

Despite Betty's growing fame, no one knew much of anything about her, except that she was a food expert from a flour company, who claimed to be a friend. Husted was discerningly skilled at balancing the mysteries of Betty with the familiar. To help deflect attention from the details of Betty's biography, Husted (through Betty) encouraged listeners to make Betty's program their own program—in essence, a national conversation among women, about "women's concerns." Predating the *Dear Abby* newspaper column by decades, Betty read listeners' letters on air and solicited their responses. "Please don't let me do all the planning," she encouraged readers in a 1927 autumn broadcast.

> *Write to me anytime—give me your suggestions for the subjects you would like discussed in these talks. Tell me your special problems—perhaps I can help. Send me your ideas, for I'm sure you can help me from the wealth of your experience.*

What emerged was a growing fascination with love in relation to food. These themes were the basis for Betty's popular hardcover recipe booklet, "15 Ways to a Man's Heart by Betty Crocker," suggesting that at least one of those ways might be cake. In one 1928 radio program, Betty Crocker reminded listeners of the husband-keeping power of her fudge cake recipe, eliciting this response: "I don't make your fudge cake [recipe] because I like white cake, but my neighbor does. Is there any danger of her capturing my husband?"

Husted was fond of relating this anecdote at home economics seminars and women's club meetings as proof that romance sells. Homemakers would politely inquire about a delicious-sounding cake recipe, but a recipe coupled with Cupid generated responses by the thousands.

Your Betty Crocker

"You can do it and I can help you" was Betty's resolute validation. Betty's message—that women at home were exactly where they were needed most—was hardly novel, but her delivery was.

In her 1927 season finale, Betty bid her "friends" farewell for the summer:

> And now in closing I want to tell you how rich I feel in all the unseen friends the radio has brought me. This season ends with this talk. The Gold Medal Flour Company has asked me to thank you for the interest you have taken in my efforts to serve you. I hope that I have been able to bring to each one of you what we consider the most important service of all—a thorough understanding of the necessity for the highest quality Kitchen-tested Flour for all your baking. Your loyalty and interest have been the greatest inspiration to me. May we always be friends.

Betty Crocker won far more notice for her innovative recipes than for her theatrical flair. Yet the performance aspect of her radio shows is often overlooked. Like the most sought-after celebrity, Betty was simultaneously accessible and aloof, appearing to have it all, do it all, and be slightly above it all.

Chapter Two

Betty Goes Hollywood

Rocks

They should be soft, not hard! To keep them that way, store in air-tight container.

1 cup soft shortening (half butter)	½ tsp. salt
1½ cups brown sugar (packed)	1 tsp. soda
3 eggs	2 tsp. cinnamon
3 cups *sifted* GOLD MEDAL Flour	1 tsp. cloves
	1 cup seedless raisins
	1 cup chopped nuts

Heat oven to 375°. Mix thoroughly shortening, brown sugar, eggs. Sift dry ingredients together and stir in. Add raisins, nuts. Drop with teaspoon about 2" apart onto greased baking sheet. Bake *8 to 10 min. Makes about 5 dozen.*

From *Gold Medal Jubilee, Select Recipes, 1880–1955:*
A treasury of favorite recipes modernized by Betty Crocker

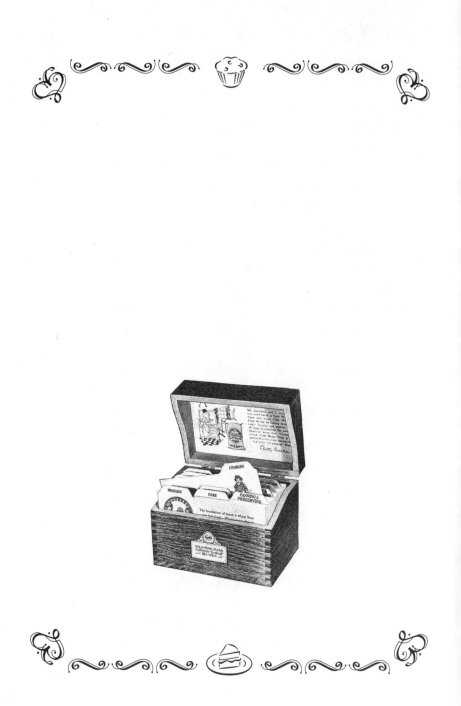

By 1930, radio listeners could dial in Betty Crocker's *Gold Medal Home Service Talks* from thirty-six stations on the NBC network, several mornings a week. But Betty wasn't the only broadcaster chatting about food, recipes, and family. Food-related companies were quick to ride the radio waves into homes across the nation. With radios in two of every five U.S. homes by 1931, radio advertising dollars reached 31 million people, even as the Great Depression worsened. "The radio, it seems to me, is primarily an invention for the benefit of woman," wrote home economist Christine Frederick for *Good Housekeeping:*

> *Its greatest achievement is banishing isolation . . . isolation, whether mental or geographical, has been the cause of much of woman's restlessness and has done more to retard her progress than any other one factor. The important problem now is to find out how the radio can best utilize the possibilities it opens up as a means of service to woman and her family.*

Taking its cue from Betty Crocker's success, the Heinz Company launched a Home Economics Department in 1930. "Announcing a New Help in Solving the Housewives' Problems," declared a Heinz ad in *Ladies' Home Journal.* A Miss Josephine Gibson was promised to lecture to thousands of visiting women "in the big auditorium at Pittsburgh," "answer any question directed at her" by mail, and to broadcast, "direct from the Home Economics Model Kitchen of H. J. Heinz Company," every

Tuesday and Friday at 10:45 in the morning, also on the NBC Network.

"For your pleasure," Hostess introduced the "Happy Wonder Bakers," who sang on the radio every Wednesday evening, along with Frank Black (NBC's musical director) and his orchestra. With a "Yo-Ho! Ho-Yo!," the Bakers and their musical accompaniment (renamed the Wonder Bakers Orchestra) quickly moved to Tuesday evenings. Hostess made entertainment available with the flip of a switch, while dessert could be had for just a quarter (for the Hostess Cocoanut Layer Cake), or even a nickel (for two Hostess Cup Cakes).

"New Radio Thrills" arrived in the fall of 1930 from Quaker Oats, who in October rolled out "The Radio Program Every One's Talking About. While you're eating your breakfast of Aunt Jemima pancakes, tune in on the Quaker Man. Every weekday morning at 8:00 to 8:15." The very next month, the Quaker Man was down for double duty: "And don't miss the coast to coast evening program at 7:30."

The competition continued to heat up with new radio programs aimed at stealing some of Betty Crocker's thunder. In 1933, General Foods invited women to "Tune in on General Foods Baking Day. Complete course in home-baking conducted by Frances Lee Barton, famous Swans Down cake-maker. Every Thursday, 11:15 AM, Eastern Standard Time, over WEAF and 35 associated N.B.C. stations. Listen in next Thursday!" Mary Lee Taylor for Pet Milk and Mary Ellis Ames for Pillsbury's Best Flour also chimed in, but to no avail. Throughout the 1930s, rival radio cooks came and went, while Betty remained a constant. Not a one of her competitors, it seemed, could match the charm that Betty, and even her very name, seemed to emanate.

Despite the nation's mounting economic troubles, Betty's radio shows flourished. By 1933, around 250,000 on-air students registered for her *Cooking School of the Air.* The same year marked the unemployment of over 14 million workers, or close to 30 percent of a labor force of 47 million. Of that 47 million, 40 million to 42 million normally worked full-time in support of a population of 122 million. With so many men out of work, some whiled away the hours in the comfort of Betty's company:

> *May an unemployed husband join your cooking school of the air? If so, I would like to join. Perhaps you think this is a bit odd, but I have been out of work almost a year. However, I am fortunate enough to have a good wife who is employed and has been ever since we were married. In the meantime, I have been doing the housework and the cooking. I was always able to get a meal [together], but since listening to you over the air, there is not the sameness over and over again. My wife told me I was a good cook, but now she says I am still better. If that is true, the credit belongs to you and not me.*

*

> *If you ever enroll old men in your cooking school, kindly enroll me. Will be 75 years in March, but don't feel any older than when I was 50. White hair puts the old men on the shelf and the result, no employment. You gave a recipe for Pumpkin Pie in the fall, if you have it on a card, kindly send me a copy.*

A failing economy meant that more and more Americans were skimping on essential food items. In 1932, the American Red Cross distributed more than 8.5 million barrels of flour to 5,140,855 families representing nearly every county nationwide.

Between 1929 and 1932, the average income of the American family fell 40 percent, from $2,300 to $1,500, of which food costs demanded approximately 25 percent. Dr. Julius Klein, assistant secretary of commerce, helpfully pointed out that this ratio was kinder than in other world population centers—"Asia spends ninety per cent of her earnings for food, and ten per cent for the comforts of life; Europe eighty per cent for food and twenty per cent for comforts; while the United States spends thirty per cent for food and seventy per cent for comforts"—but meal planning was far from easy for women struggling to feed their families on spartan budgets. Homemakers writing to Betty named grocery bill management as their biggest problem.

> *Like millions of other husbands, mine had to take a severe cut in salary and oh, Miss Crocker, sometimes I become so discouraged.*

*

> *My husband is just barely making a living for my four children and myself. He has had his wages cut terribly. I must try and do something.*

*

> *Of course you can't realize how it is when your savings are almost gone and now your home is at stake and you have to smile and try to make a meal out of nothing so your loved one will keep up the fight and not lose hope and courage; so I thought perhaps you might be able to scour up tempting, nourishing menus (that is, something out of almost nothing) so the thousands of women situated as we are, may help fight this Depression War and keep up a stiff upper lip for all.*

*

  52

*I used to be enrolled in your cooking schools of the air when
I lived in Springfield. Then hard times hit this family and
we moved to the farm . . . I had to sell my radio and G.E. refrigerator. I sure do miss them . . . What I want to ask you is,
would it be too much trouble for you to send me some of
your recipes that you have given out within the past year?*

Every day, thousands of pleas for help flooded the fledgling General Mills, Inc., established in 1928 by the merger of several
mills including Washburn Crosby. The pace in the General Mills
Home Service Department would have seemed especially familiar to I.R.T. Smith, who had been executive mail clerk at the
White House since 1897. Of the letters received by the Roosevelts during the Depression, Smith said, "I have never seen
anything like it. I used to be able to get along with two or
three assistants. Now I have twenty-two and they are all over-
worked. . . . Well, the average is seven thousand letters a day, and
that includes Sunday."

Like the President, whose influential "Fireside Chats" moved
one critic to dub him "the best broadcaster known in America
today," Betty Crocker answered her queries not only by post, but
on the radio. Her blend of you-can-do-it optimism and practical
advice was precisely what her public wanted. One listener
praised her talents: "I want to tell you that I enjoy your talks far
more than those of any other home economist program on the
air. Your talks have a real person-to-person feeling that is absent
from the other radio cooking shows." By mid-decade, two of
Betty's weekly broadcasts focused exclusively on recipes and
menus designed for families on relief.

In a June 1, 1932, radio broadcast, Betty explained how "thrift
can be made easy" by restyling leftovers:

Thrift has always been the banner of house-wifely skill and in these days of financial strain everyone is trying to avoid waste of every kind. Scraps of vegetable and bits of meat, which in a time of plenty might have been discarded, must return to the table again, to go just a little bit further. So even the least experienced cook won't want to be feeding the garbage can at the expense of her husband.

Opinion makers continued to marvel at the far-reaching Betty Crocker radio community: "While the wise farmer's wife turns the dial on her radio in Dallas County, Texas, the Minneapolis bride of a few months tunes in on the same morning program in her small city apartment—the experienced cook and the beginning, both seeking new ideas and new inspiration to help plan and prepare the universal three meals a day." But critical approval paled in comparison to heartfelt listener appreciation.

Your recipes are more within our means than most recipes are; they are economical and yet very good. It is a nice little visit in our home every time you come in over the radio.

*

I tried your muffin recipe and found it delicious. My husband doesn't usually care for muffins but he literally devoured these. "You know," he said, "the recipes you get from Betty Crocker are worth the price we paid for the radio." I agree heartily and he doesn't know the half of it. He doesn't know about all the inspiration and help I get for my homemaking.

*

Your talks, Betty Crocker, have given me hope.

For a week's worth of rabbit recipes, Betty Crocker suggests: *"Having Guests On Sunday?* Rabbit Pie • *Like Hearty Fare On Monday?* Rabbit Fricassee • *Southern Fare For Tuesday?* Rabbit Creole • *Dining Home On Wednesday?* Rabbit Curry • *Something New for Thursday?* Rabbit in Tomato Sauce • *Friends In On Friday?* Rabbit Cutlet • *Family Dinner Saturday?* Hassenpfeffer No. 1." Circa mid 1930s.

   55

The radio broadcasts were just one part of Betty Crocker's national relief service. In a free brochure, "Meal Planning on Minimum and Low Cost Budgets," Betty Crocker discussed how to procure nutritious food on Depression-era wages and maximize relief staples on the lowest budget possible. Reported one of the thousands who followed her advice:

> *Now we live on a budget and far more economical and much more tempting and appetizing meals, thanks to you, my dear. You make things so easy and your products are so sure, I never fear to take anything. . . . You surely have our votes unanimously for our good, wholesome, tempting, economical meals.*

Some of Betty's loyal listeners confided personal details that were nothing short of astonishing.

> *I hesitate just a wee bit to tell you what I'm going to now, for it makes a difference in the way people feel towards me sometimes. You see Betty Crocker, I am a blind girl and when people know that, they can't quite understand why I'm so interested in recipes and cookery ideas . . . for they think a blind girl is utterly helpless and should do nothing but sit and try to be as happy as possible under the circumstances. Here is the reason I'm so interested and why you have helped me so much. My mother died seven months ago and since then I have been doing all the housework and cooking for my two brothers and father.*

One grateful mother was moved to make Betty a part of the family—until fate intervened.

   56

*I have wanted to write for some time now. I have just had
my third son born to me on November 16. I was so sure it
was going to be a girl and we were going to call her Betty
because you have helped me so very much in making my
home a success. I had to settle for the name of Teddy.*

"Meal Planning on Minimum and Low-Cost Budgets," as well as
the recipes from the *Cooking School of the Air,* were saving
graces for many Americans. Betty Crocker's sound dietary advice won national recognition among nutritionists and social
workers. The Gold Medal Home Service Department also contributed to the National Recovery Administration (NRA) by
composing and distributing low-cost menu brochures and con-
ducting free nutrition classes and cooking demonstrations.
James Gray, whose history of General Mills was published in
1954, chronicled Betty's Depression-era service:

*It should be pointed out, as a comment on the character of
Betty Crocker as citizen, that her response to the public
plea for help was spontaneous and unselfish. The use of her
skills to advertise General Mills and to serve the miller's
enlightened self-interest was a secondary importance. In
her mind—the collective mind of the Home Service Department—it was almost an afterthought.*

Developing low-cost recipes was no small undertaking, even for
Betty Crocker's staff. Husted was famous for her standard line,
"Would you serve this in your own home?" To ensure the necessary affirmative, seemingly limitless resources were allocated for
researching, creating, testing and retesting every conceivable
way of ruining a recipe: underbaking, overbaking, omitting in-

   57

gredients, using a pan of the wrong size, baking at the wrong temperature.

Betty Knows Best

Betty Crocker's 1930s may be best remembered as her altruistic decade, but that trademark charm of hers never stopped working. In 1930, as the nation's economic woes bore down in earnest, the "noted Cooking Authority" was in the midst of a "Gold Medal National Exhibition of Foods Men Like." A continuation of the "Kitchen-tested" concept ads begun in the 1920s, these latest recipes were "A Revelation in Easier Home Baking." Recent "scientific developments in flour milling" yielded spectacular kitchen achievements: "467 Women Baked This 'Difficult' Yorkshire Pudding, with a Record of 462 Perfect Results. Only 5 Missed Perfect Success Their First Try!" The campaign continued—recipe number 5 was a "Kris Kringle Stollen" that "Men Can't Get Enough Of"—with an invitation from Betty Crocker to send in 10 cents for the "'15 Ways to a Man's Heart' Recipe Set Containing 15 Simplified Recipes." Try them, Betty explained, "if you would like to hear your husband say—'My wife is the greatest cook in the world.'"

The innovations of some great cooks might have been long forgotten if not for Betty. According to company lore, a General Mills executive named Carl Smith took a 1930 train trip into baking history. Traveling on Southern Pacific's Portland–San Francisco line, Smith ordered a late dinner. When fresh, hot biscuits were served with the meal, Smith knew the railroad chef had solved a longtime mystery: how to keep shortening fresh and the leavening agent active long after the ingredients are combined.

  58

Bisquick flour was popular with homemakers starting in 1931. Throughout the next two decades, Betty Crocker's staff created thousands of Bisquick recipes.

   59

The General Mills chemists worked with the concept—and created Bisquick, which came on the market in 1931 with great fanfare.

"The name of this marvelous new food invention is Bisquick —B-I-S-Q-U-I-C-K. And the way it acts borders on the miraculous." Bisquick's special features were almost too numerous to mention, but Betty was more than up to the task. First came the technical innovations: "The 'knack' or 'trick' of perfect biscuits is made *into* it. By an amazing, newly discovered process of mixing the shortening and dry ingredients." Next came the ease of making shortcake biscuits in "90 seconds from package to oven," so simple *"even a child* can't go wrong." Last came the sweet reward: "And—look for a kiss and a compliment from your husband." All this cost just the price of a postage stamp—plus one Bisquick top, or 25 cents—with Betty Crocker's "101 Delicious Bisquick Creations."

Just as Betty proclaimed, "Millions of women everywhere are abandoning pet recipes in favor of this wonderful new Bisquick way. Try it. You'll say it's as easy as A-B-C." Bisquick was also perfectly positioned to ride the 1930s culinary craze for waffles. In January 1933, *McCall's* recommended serving this treat "if you want to cause a sensation at the luncheon or tea table." Waffles made by adding milk and eggs to Bisquick "are like something from heaven—light as a feather . . . gold as Autumn . . . good as the magic of Betty Crocker can make them."

Betty made it impossible for homemakers to forget the ease and convenience of Bisquick. "Remember the name—spelled B-I-S-Q-U-I-C-K," she instructed. "Avoid cheap substitutes." And no need for substitutes, with Bisquick newly packaged in "Bride's size—makes 40 Bisquicks," and "Family size—makes 80 Bisquicks."

  60

That's Entertainment

To Betty, home baking meant endless hours of fun. But one of her competitors, "Mrs. Alice Adams Proctor" of New York City's Continental Baking Company—owner of the Hostess brand— meant to liberate Betty and her acolytes from the kitchen once and for all. "There are always things to do nowadays that are more fun—and more important—than baking cake. So why bake when you can *buy* cake like this Hostess Cocoanut Layer—rich, delicious, tender as any homemade cake?" For 25 cents, "You couldn't make such rich, good cake as this for anything like the price—and that doesn't even count your time and labor."

In the face of these convenient, cheap foods with "fun" built in to the purchase price, General Mills needed to keep ahead of the competition. Gold Medal Flour and Bisquick recipes alone were not enough to maintain Betty Crocker brand loyalty. But $5,000 in cash just might do the trick.

The Betty Crocker Cake Naming Contest of 1933 delivered the good news. "Now at last—a contest which even the average woman can enter and win! You don't even have to make the cake! Just make up a name for it." Nine hundred thirty-six cash prizes—from a $1,000 first prize down to $2—would be awarded. "Don't say you can't win," Betty urged, "until you have at least read the instructions. Now this is no ordinary contest. It is not a word-building struggle, nothing that will take much time. . . . Any name that is descriptive of the cake or seems especially appropriate will have a good opportunity to win the first prize" for naming this "cocoanut-orange" layer cake.

Gold-N-Sno took top honors in the Cake Naming Contest, but the real prize was Betty's in the form of a new show called "Letters Brought to Life." Starting in 1931, broadcast-worthy letters

A cake named Gold-N-Sno won first prize.

were developed into scripts with a "service angle of drama." In one episode, "Not So Dumb," Betty Crocker set the scene:

> *Hello Everybody! A recent survey discloses that the fact that out of 11,000,000 women between the ages of 15 and 44, one out of every three is employed. Isn't that an amazing figure! It seems even more amazing when you consider that a great number of these women are holding down two jobs—and many of them are married, and come to the big important job of homemaking—keeping a husband well fed, etc. The question is: Can the average woman do both jobs, and do them well?*
>
> *Our Letters Brought to Life today tells the story of a young woman who had to answer that question under rather dramatic circumstances. . . .*

The drama begins with Ken, a frantic lawyer who is desperate for clerical help before a big court case. A plucky stenographer, Dunn, suggests to Ken's wife, Nancy, that she come to the office to work for Ken. At first Nancy resists serving Ken both in and out of the home. After some debate between the women, Dunn reveals that she, too, is married and manages to balance both worlds with the help of Betty Crocker's brochure "Seven Golden Rules for Business Housekeepers." By the end, Nancy is convinced that she can also tend "both burners" and expresses gratitude for Dunn's advice.

Encouraged by popular response to the story of Ken and Nancy, and tales of couples like them, Betty Crocker devoted substantial broadcast time to the philosophy of attracting and keeping a mate. In one series, she invited eligible bachelors and bachelorettes to the microphone. Listeners couldn't quite agree on the perfect plan for love and marriage.

Here's a new slant on your "what do we want in wives" controversy. We ["two satisfied bachelors"] can and do very well cooking anything the average good housewife can cook. Possibly show them a recipe or two. We wash our own undies and sox. Make our own bed and scrub our floor. We entertain nice young ladies and won't let them do the dishes. We enjoy life and don't have to account for being out after 9 p.m. We're satisfied and don't want any wives to get in our way. Further, we're both in our late twenties and have been going this way for the past 10 years with the exception of the two years we both tried wives. It didn't last and were we glad to get back together. Yes, we use Gold Medal Flour and we'd like to invite you to dinner.

*

I get a kick out of your interviews with the young men of marriageable ages. I imagine some of them will stay single for a long time.

*

I want you to know how perfect your fall cooking school was broadcasted. Your interviews with eligible young men on what men want in the women they marry was most enlightening and it does give inspiration to live a little more romantically when we are given a few ideas to live up to, and knowing that it is what the men really want after all.

*

I can't say that I care much for your talks about what different men want in their [future] wives. Most of us who listen

Betty Crocker promoted the partnership between General Mills and local bakers by suggesting that homemakers order her "glorious cake."

   65

are married and our husbands have all they're going to get, unless it's some different food, for which you are giving us recipes in that time. Besides we all know they won't get what they are looking for. They'll fall in love with some pretty nitwit and won't even stop to ask whether or not she can cook!

Some listeners clustered around the proverbial back fence to exchange gossip about those housewives whose skills weren't quite up to the Betty Crocker standard.

I feel sorry for some of the young men I see getting married. They are getting wives who can't cook or manage home. One of my girl friends has a wonderful husband, but she doesn't care about cooking or making a home either. I have told her if she didn't change, she would lose him and so has her own mother. If she used Gold Medal products it would lighten her tasks and make homemaking and meal planning real fun instead of drudgery.

*

I always enjoy your talks so much, especially your interviews with young men. Some of them certainly expect a whole lot of the girls they expect to marry some day. I wonder what the girls think about it? Well, I think all girls should know how to cook, before they get married, and I am sure if they listen to your talks they will receive some very valuable information.

*

I enjoy your talks on what kind of girl men shall like to marry. It calls to mind the many little defects in our home-making and appearance, which we are only too happy to

improve on. Your talk is like a spiritual mirror, where we
can see our defects. I am doing lots better in many things.

Betty's most popular bachelor interview series highlighted men
of various professions: "The Mechanic Wants a Smiling Wife";
"The Girl the Farmer Dreams Of"; "The Ideal of the Young Advertising Man"; "The Young Doctor Describes the Wife He
Wants." One show, "The Girl the Football Hero Is Looking For,"
elicited a barrage of mail from Betty's loyal listeners. The football
player informed Betty and the nation that he dreamed of an old-
fashioned wife who would keep house like his mother—frugally
and without any electrical appliances. Some of the responses to
his wish list:

> *The football star, to my way of thinking, is an unmitigated*
> *ass. I certainly hope no girl ever ruins her life by marrying*
> *him.*

*

> *What a selfish, conceited football hero you chose to inter-*
> *view. Whew! Didn't like a thing about him. Made me cross*
> *all day just knowing he is alive . . .*

*

> *From what I see and hear from the girls of today, your foot-*
> *ball man will have some trouble finding his girl. His kind*
> *are rather scarce, but I think he has the right idea.*

In "A Word to the Wives," Betty interviewed husbands about
food, and its place in the experience of domestic bliss. This series, with its helpful hints designed to create harmonious households and to keep husbands from straying, was geared toward
young women of marriageable age. Betty Crocker's words of

wisdom inspired wide-ranging responses from brides, would-be brides, and nonbrides of all ages.

I can't begin to tell you how much I have enjoyed your broadcasts. I must admit that these last few broadcasts have rather set me wondering, "Isn't there something I could do to make my husband more comfortable around his own fireside?"

*

Your new series of talks and helps are stunning in their originality and oh, so exciting and reviving the old desire to please.

*

Please send me a carbon copy of the husband you broadcasted this morning.

*

I too think husbands should tell wives of their good points more. Most of them never fail to tell them their faults.

*

I enjoy your little talks so much and I might say although not married, and hardly expect to be, yet I keep a little apartment with my sister. And we like nice inexpensive things to eat. And, with your recipes I can manage to make our evening meal after we come home from business. So please do not think these good things you tell us are just to cater to mere men. We unclaimed blessings are just as important.

*

Do you know I think that if women were as eager to learn new ways of fixing new dishes or remodeling the old ones,

  68

as they are in new beauty aids and how to make themselves more lovely, they wouldn't have so much trouble in keeping their husbands in good humor. Not that they shouldn't keep themselves lovely.

*

I too enjoy the talks you have been giving on matrimony. Personally I believe most husbands want a loving companion first, but they also want a good cook. My husband always delights in the new dishes I make.

*

How I do enjoy your talks and suggestions that we get over the radio! Especially interesting were the talks on what men like. My mother always said the easy way to a man's heart is through his stomach. Just a plain everyday saying but quite true I think.

*

My husband is just about the best man God ever made—he don't smoke, he don't drink and don't swear, he don't use bad language and he don't ever go out without me. We have been married over 15 years, and we haven't had a quarrel, a fight or argument. He is the most unselfish person, I come first in everything! But he has a sweet tooth, he likes my cooking and baking and thinks I am about tops. When he has only one weakness, I will try to satisfy it!

*

If you really want your husband to be crazy over you just doll up, treat him rough and give him nothing. I've seen this work out too many times to ever believe anything different, even if it shouldn't be that way. So, there you have my opinion on the matter.

Sweet on Betty

Much to the entertainment of the Gold Medal Home Service staff, a number of smitten bachelors took their chances as to whether Betty Crocker was a Miss or a Mrs., and wooed her with love letters, gifts, valentines, and marriage proposals. One man confessed that he was not interested in cooking, just the cook, requesting that Betty give him some sort of sign over the radio if she too was interested. "I pride myself on being a gentleman and I have never been guilty of this sort of thing before, but your voice and manner have so appealed to me that I just could not refrain."

Husted's unfinished autobiography contains a vivid record of Betty's effect on men: "Many men wrote in. They would listen to radio on their way to jobs or because it was such a novelty that they would make a point of listening in the morning. The letters were often humorous, but also some were quite serious when they said they would like to marry Betty Crocker—or would like her to consider them because they were eager for a wife who could cook."

Though the lovelorn never got anywhere with Betty, her staff were not always quite so aloof. Wrote one gentleman with nothing to lose, "Dear Madame, I should be pleased to have one of your recipe booklets as per announcement on the radio. I wonder would it be possible to include a good cook to prepare it for me? I am a lonely widower and am in need of a good companion. Thank you in advance." An attached memo from one Betty Crocker staff member to another reads, "Don't turn this one down! I will get you a hubby yet!"

Correspondences occasionally sprang up between Betty Crocker staff members and lonely bachelors—and at least one re-

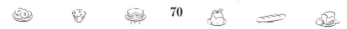

sulted in marriage. News of the union leaked to the press, leading to false rumors that Betty was ending her radio career to get married. In response, General Mills took out a full-page magazine ad and devoted radio time to setting the record straight with Betty's adoring public. On air, Betty Crocker commented:

I was afraid last spring that you might think I wouldn't be back on the air with you this year, because the newspaper printed something about Betty Crocker getting married. That was all a mistake. The girl who was married was a former member of our staff, but Betty Crocker is right here as usual. Instead of practicing making biscuits for a husband, I'm afraid I will have to be content to keep doing my cooking in the GOLD MEDAL Kitchen so that we can work out all these recipes for you. I have loads of fun doing my work here in our GOLD MEDAL Home Service Department and

From *Betty Crocker's Dinner for Two Cookbook.*

nothing could give me more satisfaction than to hear, as I often do, that I am helping you with your housekeeping problems.

Betty's charms were a counterweight to the cares of the Great Depression. Her beguiling manner lifted the spirits of millions—just as her message won their loyalty. As Eleanor Roosevelt wrote in 1933, "Perhaps one of the real blessings of the depression is that we are beginning to find out that there are things in the world worth doing and that we do not have to waste time."

Hooray for Hollywood!

In 1934, Will Hays, the head of the Motion Picture Producers and Distributors of America, reflected on the film industry's effect on its times: "No medium has contributed more greatly than the film to the maintenance of the national morale." Even at the Depression's depths, 60 million to 80 million Americans attended the movies each week, developing an intense and lasting love affair with Hollywood and its real-life cast of celebrities. General Mills, too, saw its future in Hollywood, and made plans to send Betty Crocker—Husted—west to meet film stars. An insider's peek into the domestic lives of celebrities was a provocative twist for the heretofore kitchen-bound Betty.

In 1933, Husted approached Metro-Goldwyn-Mayer Pictures (MGM) and later Paramount and Warner Bros. studios, all of which agreed to let Betty Crocker interview their contracted stars. MGM, quick to recognize the crossover appeal of Betty Crocker, staged many publicity outings. Escorted by studio executives, Husted/Crocker enjoyed cocktail parties, sightseeing trips, luncheons, yachting excursions, and movie debuts. Soon she had free access to closed movie sets and permission to interview anyone she cared to, including the studio's cooking staff, about Hollywood fare. "In addition to her fame as an actress," Betty learned, Joan Crawford—who, not unlike Betty Crocker, got her stage name as the result of a contest (this one had been devised by MGM's Louis B. Mayer)—"is known in Hollywood for her clever home management. She plans all her own menus."

Movie stars and studio heads found Husted as Betty irresistible, and several invited her home to meet their families. Betty Crocker became something of a media darling, posing for publicity photos around town. One shot shows Husted poolside, dressed in a long polka-dot dress and holding a frying pan, with swimsuit-clad Hollywood starlets surrounding her. Then as now, there was nothing "Hollywood" about Betty Crocker, but her novelty was universal, even in Tinseltown.

After a summer hiatus in 1936, Husted spiced up Betty's radio broadcasts with stories from her California adventures. However, Hollywood did not go to Betty's head. Dispensing with celebrity dish, she portrayed movie stars as real people who just happened to have high-profile careers. Many of Betty's Hollywood-themed broadcasts centered on the fact that Hollywood folk ate food, just like the rest of the nation—only they ate less of it. In one such broadcast series, "Question Box," Betty warned of the dangers of crash dieting:

There is no place in the country where you run into so many wild theories about food as you do in Hollywood. I met a charming girl in Hollywood this summer who was the temporary victim of the baked potato and skim milk diet. . . . She did look sort of woebegone after a few days of that monotonous fare, that it seemed cruel to let her go on.

   73

Betty explained how she sat the young actress down and taught her the importance of a balanced diet. Next, Betty counseled her audience to ignore fad diets and follow the lead of Norma Shearer, a sensible and nutritionally sound actress:

> *So I advise, instead of eating a small amount of vegetables and fruits, and then "going to town" on the desserts and candy, tip the balance the other way; fill up the "aching void" with more vegetables, green salads, fruits, light soups, etc. And go mightily careful on the sweets or rich foods. But don't forget the exercise, and don't leave out the plain simple foods in the required daily food list. And enjoy good meals! Why, what do you suppose Norma Shearer's favorite Sunday breakfast is? Pancakes, sausage and green salad. Doesn't that sound good to you?*

Betty Crocker's radio broadcasts overflowed with stories about the eating and cooking habits of screen stars, among them Gloria Swanson, Mary Pickford, Jean Hersholt, Robert Young, Cary Grant, Dolores del Rio, and Dick Powell. In a 1937 broadcast, Betty recalled her visit with Greta Garbo's leading man during a break in the filming of *Camille*:

> *Of course I asked Robert Taylor about his food interests, and he was very amusing about that. I'll tell you what he said on Friday, when I give you the recipe for his favorite food, Lemon Meringue Pie—the kind his mother makes! But I will tell you now that he said, "I like good plain foods." And I think that's true of most men, don't you? And that's why we put so many recipes for good plain food in our recipes folders that are packed in each sack of Gold*

15th ANNIVERSARY 1921 1936

Betty Crocker's

15

PRIZE RECIPES

favorites of each year – 1921 to 1936

★

Betty's prize recipes included stand-out favorites: Streusel-filled Coffee Cake (1923), Pineapple Upside Down Cake (1924), Lemon Meringue Pie (1928), Pigs in Blankets (1933), and Favorite Fudge Cake (1936).

   75

Vitality
DEMANDS ENERGY

109 SMART NEW WAYS TO SERVE
BREAD
OUR OUTSTANDING ENERGY FOOD

Physicians, the Secretary of the Committee on Foods of the American Medical Association, Emily Post, Oscar of the Waldorf, and actresses Sylvia Sidney, Claudette Colbert, and Margaret Sullavan gave bread their endorsements in Betty Crocker's "Vitality Demands Energy" (1934).

   76

*Medal "Kitchen-tested" Flour. And I think if you all watch
for these recipes folders, they will help keep your men folk
happy—for you'll find that they contain recipes for delicious pies, cakes, muffins and meat dishes, too, that will be
favorites with the men.*

The subject of fame blended smoothly with Betty's traditional
mix of food and love, as Betty's Hollywood shows included news
about celebrities juggling diet, exercise, and home life with Hollywood careers. Betty never missed an opportunity to inquire
about celebrities' love lives and solicit their views on the ingredients of a successful marriage. (Robert Taylor "didn't feel competent to talk about women in any way.") Betty didn't waver from
her belief that good food could improve even the best of rela-
tionships.

Studios extended Husted repeat invitations for visits, interviews, and joint promotions. Betty Crocker became a publicity
must for high-profile celebrities like Bette Davis, Joan Crawford,
Jean Harlow, Bing Crosby, Helen Hayes, and the young Elizabeth Taylor. Celebrities' favorite recipes were a hit among Betty
Crocker's followers, especially Clark Gable's wife's recipe for
Coconut Cake, Irene Dunne's recipe for Kentucky Nut Cake,
and Robert Taylor's mother's recipe for Lemon Meringue Pie.
One listener wrote to Betty, "The Clark Gable frosting sounded
very intriguing. I can't imagine a movie star's wife working in a
kitchen baking a real cake!"

Intense scientific research into the properties of vitamins increasingly had the side effect of inspiring fad diets that linked
bread to weight gain and this created bad publicity for flour
companies. General Mills deployed Hollywood darling Betty
Crocker on damage control. Husted recruited slender actresses—

Claudette Colbert, Margaret Sullavan, and Sylvia Sidney—to endorse bread as a foundation for a healthy and nutritious diet. The celebrities were featured in Betty Crocker's 1935 national campaign and booklet, "Bread for Vitality." In exchange for their endorsements, the celebrities received free publicity for their latest cinematic feats. For example, Claudette Colbert, winner of the 1934 Best Actress Oscar for *It Happened One Night,* was identified as the "star of Cecil B. DeMille's new Paramount spectacle *Cleopatra.*" Next to her photograph appeared testimony that bread provided much of her abundant energy. Fans were urged to read Claudette's personal letter:

> *Dear Betty Crocker,*
> *You can't imagine the strain of film work. Without plenty of vitality, a person simply can't make a go of it—can't keep looking her best. Diet, of course is tremendously important—and I've always been told bread is the best food for energy. I love bread—always have it in some form, three times a day.*

Elmer McCollum, a professor at Johns Hopkins who was America's leading nutrition researcher, and the Yale vitamin expert Lafayette Mendel joined Betty Crocker and her Hollywood coterie on a 1934 radio special highlighting the healthful properties of white bread as a diet food. McCollum further championed General Mills' cause with a 1935 letter to Congress denouncing "the pernicious teachings of food faddists who have sought to make people afraid of white-flour bread."

Betty was not the only home economist making the Hollywood circuit, but she was the one who commanded Hollywood's attention. The studios collaborated with General Mills on a se-

Hollywood stars shared their favorite Bisquick recipes with Betty Crocker in "How to Take a Trick a Day with Bisquick."

79

Betty Crocker and your BAKER
S<u>HARE</u> this triumph!

13-*egg* Angel Food

"Please get your baker friends to make your wonderful 13-egg Angel Food for us again . . . now!" said countless women to Betty Crocker. "The *perfect* angel cake! And think what a lovely cool dessert . . . with ice cream or fruit."

A triumph last fall . . . when three million women bought it, for the first time, from leading bakers. Even more of a triumph now . . . baked for you, fresh every day this week, by *your baker!* A masterpiece that proves the power of this magic combination: the talents of the world's foremost home cooking authority, Betty Crocker, who created the recipe . . . and the scientific facilities and professional skill of your baker who is baking it for

you now. An angel food of infinite delicacy. Of dream lightness . . . high, fluffy, moist, and fine. So tender there isn't the slightest pull. Exquisitely flavored. Clear radiant white inside, with a delicious golden brown macaroon-like crust.

Your baker is making this heavenly angel food for you . . . fresh every day this week! . . . from Betty Crocker's famous 13-egg recipe. He is using Gold Medal Softasilk Cake Flour, the whites of 13 fresh eggs, and the other high quality ingredients you would use yourself in your own kitchen. A triumph for you when you serve it.

Let your baker do the work! The easiest way to supply your family with the variety of wheat foods they need

is to use the services of your professional baker. He knows the kind of baked foods you like. New recipe ideas as well as expert baking information are given him continuously by General Mills' Products Control. Betty Crocker's cooperation with bakers on this 13-egg Angel Food is just one more instance of the value of Products Control to bakers.

Your family will relish this 13-egg Angel Food any way you serve it.

Order it today from your baker direct or through your grocer!

THIS SEAL
attached to the cake wrapper is your guarantee that the cake is baked according to Betty Crocker's famous "Kitchen-tested" recipe.

*Above—*The ice cream sandwich glorified! Generous slice of ice cream between 2 fluffy pieces of 13-egg Angel Food . . . proudly topped with rich dark bitter-sweet chocolate sauce.

*Left—*Ripe red berries nestling in billowed whipped cream on a slice of 13-egg Angel Food. Another delightful, refreshing, summer's day dessert.

GENERAL MILLS · INC.
A NATION-WIDE FLOUR MILLING ORGANIZATION COMPRISING 21 MILLS HAVING 87,600 BARREL DAILY CAPACITY

Let your BAKER do your baking

Betty Crocker magazine ad, 1933.

   80

ries of recipe booklets. In "Let the Stars Show You How to Take a Trick a Day with Bisquick" and "Betty Crocker's 101 Delicious Bisquick Creations," Betty showcased recipes and serving ideas from "smart luminaries of movieland" as well as from celebrity chefs, socialites, and magazine columnists. These inexpensive booklets covered topics from emergency meals for unexpected guests, to thrift menus and ideas for dressing up leftovers, to tips for the hostess of tennis, golf, yachting, and hunting luncheons.

Bette Davis recommended recipes for Bisquick hunt club sandwiches and ginger waffles. Joan Crawford, known for her "Smart Dinners," favored whole-wheat Bisquick rolls and potatoes on the half shell with avocado salad. Claudette Colbert offered her Bisquick recipe for peach shortcake, and Bing Crosby gave his wife's menu for a "Southern Plantation Supper," complete with Bisquick fried chicken, corn fritters, spoon bread, candied sweet potatoes, and chocolate icebox cake.

Betty's celebrity connections landed her a home away from home, and she was the perfect resident of a place where nothing is as it seems. Husted's Hollywood personification of Betty Crocker was so convincing that her own identity became curiously intertwined and interchangeable with Betty's. Betty's Hollywood friends, expert as they were at playing a role, certainly distinguished between the two. But there was simply no question that "Betty Crocker at Studio Soiree" made much better copy than "The Director of General Mills' Home Service Department Mingling with Film Stars."

The stars obliged by validating Betty Crocker's mission in their own words. In one radio chat, Norma Shearer told Betty:

Of course the women who do all their own household tasks are the ones who have the greatest problem. I have the

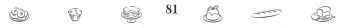

deepest admiration and respect for them. When you think they have to do everything—the cooking—the cleaning— looking after the children—why, it's about four jobs. And unfortunately, there's often not much credit in it. They don't hear about it until it's not done! Yet, there's nothing more important than bringing up children!

Basking in the esteem of their Hollywood idols, listeners reached out to their celebrity connection Betty Crocker with requests for the recipes of the stars.

"The Betty Crocker Effect" reaped enormous financial gain for General Mills. A 1940 national survey indicated that Betty Crocker's Home Service radio programs held a strong category lead, and that she received over a quarter of a million letters per year. It is no coincidence that General Mills was one of the "Golden Eight" corporations that throughout the Depression never failed to pay—without reduction—a regular dividend on common stock.

Chapter Three

On Betty's Watch

Service Cake

Cream together ⅓ **cup shortening**

¾ cup sugar

Blend in **2 eggs, well beaten**

Sift together **1½ cups** *sifted* **GOLD MEDAL Flour**

or,

1⅔ cups *sifted* **SOFTASILK**

½ tsp. salt

1¾ tsp. baking powder

Blend into creamed mixture alternately with

½ cup milk

1 tsp. vanilla

Pour into greased and floured *8-in. sq. pan.* Bake *about 35 min.* in 350° oven.

Victory Icing

(For 2-layer 8 or 9-in. cake . . . to be served soon after icing.)

Heat just to boiling   **¾ cup light corn syrup**
Pour into (in thin stream)   **2 egg whites, stiffly beaten**
Beat until fluffy.
Blend in   **Pinch of salt**
     ½ tsp. lemon extract
     ½ tsp. orange extract

From Betty Crocker's "Your Share" (1943)

As World War II swallowed the Great Depression, homemaking took on a renewed sense of urgency. In more than 30 million kitchens nationwide, women were charged with providing their families foods for building strong bodies, steady nerves, and high morale. "The eyes of the nation are upon you," President Roosevelt told American women in February 1942. "In far-flung outposts, in the military isolation of camps near home, men at sea, men in tanks, men with guns, men in planes, look to you for strength." Homemakers were urged to sign—and uphold—the U.S. government's "Consumer Pledge for Total Defense":

> *I will buy carefully.*
> *I will take good care of the things I have.*
> *I will waste nothing.*

Realizing these goals on a national scale required extensive planning and education, encouragement and enforcement. The government called for consumers and consumer product companies to forge a partnership to address a common problem: food. Prewar food expenditures averaged $14,753,000,000 per year for an abundance of consumables.

But suddenly homemakers had rationing and shortages to contend with, along with rising prices. Corporations faced scarcity of farm labor, as well as transportation and distribution problems. Ideas for how to feed families at home while conserving rations for troops abroad were in high demand.

Betty Crocker had the answers, and the national platform to deliver them. Marshaling vast informational resources with militarylike precision, General Mills' Home Service and marketing departments orchestrated elaborate public service initiatives so as to position Betty Crocker as an indispensable wartime resource. Betty was everywhere—on the radio, in women's magazines, in newspaper columns, in the mail, and in recipe booklets available in grocery stores—sending messages of empowerment and civic pride.

Betty's staff worked tirelessly to ease the pain of rationing, which was no small feat considering that sugar, a key component of the most beloved Betty Crocker recipes, was first on the government's list. Beginning in January 1942, the Office of Price Administration appointed local rationing boards. Food rationing began on May 5, 1942, with the twenty-eight-stamp "sugar book." The weekly allowance was set at eight ounces per person. Coffee, butter and other fats, canned and frozen goods, and red meat were rationed by February 1943.

In an effort to stem feelings of deprivation and resentment—and to avoid repeat price inflation rampant on the World War I home front—Betty Crocker explained the philosophy behind the program. "Food rationing at home helps to save lives of American service men." In *McCall's,* Betty rallied homemakers: "Let's make rationing work!" The "Betty Crocker Suggests" campaign offered recipes designed to do just that. Set in a column bracketed by Betty's portrait and signature and punctuated with trios of patriotic stars, the advertisements alternated menu planning advice with news items from Uncle Sam and homemakers' letters, recounting baking success à la Betty.

Sugar-saving tips figured prominently in Betty's suggestions. "No sugar required for fresh fruit shortcake!" she declared in a July 1942 ad. "Just do this: . . . Sweeten your raspberries, or strawberries, with a bit of corn syrup. Use corn syrup to sweeten

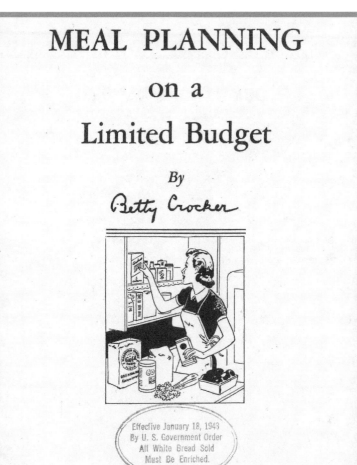

MEAL PLANNING

on a

Limited Budget

By

Betty Crocker

Effective January 18, 1943
By U. S. Government Order
All White Bread Sold
Must Be Enriched.

★ **NUTRITION FOR DEFENSE** ★

Betty lamented, in "Meal Planning on a Limited Budget" (1943), "Trying to handle the food budget economically and yet give the family the kind of meals they enjoy and the food they should have for their physical needs is a very interesting game. And I don't know of anything that brings more satisfaction to a woman."

   89

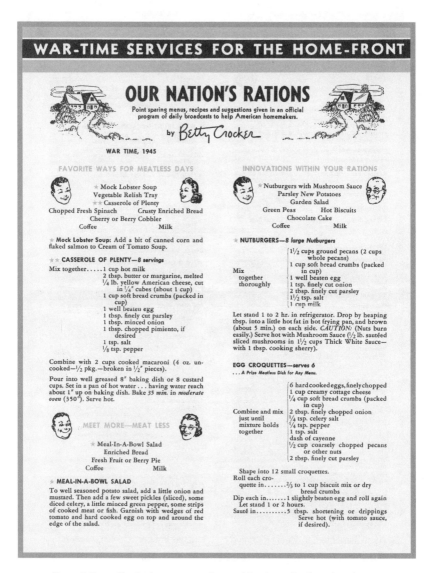

OUR NATION'S RATIONS

Point sparing menus, recipes and suggestions given in an official
program of daily broadcasts to help American homemakers.

by *Betty Crocker*

WAR TIME, 1945

FAVORITE WAYS FOR MEATLESS DAYS

★ Mock Lobster Soup
Vegetable Relish Tray
★★ Casserole of Plenty
Chopped Fresh Spinach   Crusty Enriched Bread
Cherry or Berry Cobbler
Coffee   Milk

★ **Mock Lobster Soup:** Add a bit of canned corn and flaked salmon to Cream of Tomato Soup.

★★ **CASSEROLE OF PLENTY—8 servings**

Mix together.....1 cup hot milk
2 tbsp. butter or margarine, melted
¼ lb. yellow American cheese, cut in ¼" cubes (about 1 cup)
1 cup soft bread crumbs (packed in cup)
1 well beaten egg
1 tbsp. finely cut parsley
1 tbsp. minced onion
1 tbsp. chopped pimiento, if desired
1 tsp. salt
⅛ tsp. pepper

Combine with 2 cups cooked macaroni (4 oz. uncooked—½ pkg.—broken in ½" pieces).

Pour into well greased 8" baking dish or 8 custard cups. Set in a pan of hot water . . . having water reach about 1" up on baking dish. Bake *35 min.* in *moderate oven* (350°). Serve hot.

MEET MORE—MEAT LESS

★ Meal-In-A-Bowl Salad
Enriched Bread
Fresh Fruit or Berry Pie
Coffee   Milk

★ **MEAL-IN-A-BOWL SALAD**

To well seasoned potato salad, add a little onion and mustard. Then add a few sweet pickles (sliced), some diced celery, a little minced green pepper, some strips of cooked meat or fish. Garnish with wedges of red tomato and hard cooked egg on top and around the edge of the salad.

INNOVATIONS WITHIN YOUR RATIONS

★ Nutburgers with Mushroom Sauce
Parsley New Potatoes
Garden Salad
Green Peas   Hot Biscuits
Chocolate Cake
Coffee   Milk

★ **NUTBURGERS—8 large Nutburgers**

Mix together thoroughly
1½ cups ground pecans (2 cups whole pecans)
1 cup soft bread crumbs (packed in cup)
1 well beaten egg
1 tsp. finely cut onion
2 tbsp. finely cut parsley
1½ tsp. salt
1 cup milk

Let stand 1 to 2 hr. in refrigerator. Drop by heaping tbsp. into a little hot fat in hot frying pan, and brown (about 5 min.) on each side. *CAUTION:* (Nuts burn easily.) Serve hot with Mushroom Sauce (½ lb. sautéed sliced mushrooms in 1½ cups Thick White Sauce— with 1 tbsp. cooking sherry).

EGG CROQUETTES—serves 6
. . . *A Prize Meatless Dish for Any Menu.*

Combine and mix just until mixture holds together
6 hard cooked eggs, finely chopped
1 cup creamy cottage cheese
¼ cup soft bread crumbs (packed in cup)
2 tbsp. finely chopped onion
¼ tsp. celery salt
¼ tsp. pepper
1 tsp. salt
dash of cayenne
½ cup coarsely chopped pecans or other nuts
2 tbsp. finely cut parsley

Shape into 12 small croquettes.
Roll each croquette in.......⅔ to 1 cup biscuit mix or dry bread crumbs
Dip each in.......1 slightly beaten egg and roll again
Let stand 1 or 2 hours.
Sauté in..........5 tbsp. shortening or drippings
Serve hot (with tomato sauce, if desired).

One of Betty Crocker's many wartime publications distributed to homemakers in the name of the home-front war effort.

  90

the whipped cream." And the following winter: "Now's the time to make a hit with midwinter fruit pies! . . . Canned fruit pies made the Betty Crocker way gladden hearts, save sugar." The baking secret to these recipes was General Mills' Bisquick. The product's blend of ingredients included sugar, so that the consumer needn't use her own ration.

Betty demonstrated the patriotic qualities of Bisquick biscuits in an ad quoting "Mrs. America": "He'll have his biscuits, and often. Even if I've been toiling for Red Cross or such. No trouble for me, making biscuits. Just a whisk and a pat. Absolutely a cinch, with my trusty Bisquick. Can we have 'em tomorrow, too? Of course! Simple to make." With thrift and economy key ingredients, here was a food that embodied the War Advertising Council's 1943 anti-inflation message: "Use it up. Wear it out. Make it do. Or do without."

Starve the Garbage Can

In 1942, the government called for a stockpile of a billion pounds of fats needed for war production. The launching of a single big ship required 96,000 pounds of mixed tallow, suet, and petroleum products to grease the way. And with consumers meeting just half the fats quota, Betty Crocker, along with other key spokespeople, was called upon to redouble conservation efforts. Betty created alternative baking techniques to save on butter. "IN PASTRY: Use lard or vegetable shortening. If those are not available, bacon or poultry fat, or clarified drippings may be used."

Betty spoke out in support of the national "Starve the Garbage Can" campaign with tips for conserving food, eliminating waste, and bolstering morale. "Watch Your Wasteline" seconded the "Washington Newsletter" in *McCall's* of August 1943. "Remem-

   91

ber that if every family wasted only a single slice of bread per week, the total would come to 1,000,000 loaves a year." Thrift was essential to homemakers juggling two budgets, one for money and one for ration coupons. "Save your 'blue' stamps," advised Betty Crocker, "by using fresh fruits in season when abundant and at their best—by extending canned fruits—by using dried fruits for variety."

For a company lunch "easy on points," Betty Crocker planned a meatless menu around "Green and Gold" filling (green beans and margarine) in Biscuit Rings, with "salad bowl of shredded lettuce, raw cauliflowerettes and radish discs, little extra biscuits, and jam and pickles" as side dishes, with fresh pineapple and cupcakes for dessert.

With prime meat rations reserved for military tables, civilians could look forward to eating less beef and more pork, both summer and winter. In her contribution to the search for untapped sources of nutrition, Betty Crocker invoked Uncle Sam's silver lining: "WEALTHY! 'We have great riches of wheat and other cereal grains.'" Betty's bottom line: "It's good to extend your meat with Wheaties," a General Mills cereal touted for its "good proteins."

For Betty, good eating depended on good cooking. Her staff, ever dedicated to food preparations that fit the times, titled this recipe after the national mood:

EMERGENCY STEAK

1 lb. fresh hamburger, or	*1 cup Wheaties*
ground round steak	*1 tsp. salt and ¼ tsp. pepper*
½ cup milk	*finely chopped onion (if desired)*

Broil 8-15 minutes at 500 degrees. Brown other side and finish cooking. 6 servings.

   92

With nearly half of all women employed at some point during the war, cooking time became precious. Cereal might have been an obvious choice for breakfast, but Betty suggested, "Why not Wheaties with milk for lunch or supper, occasionally?" In May 1943, Betty reminded women, "War workers in your family? Please note: Dr. Helen Mitchell, Principal Nutritionist, U.S. Health, Welfare and Defense Committee, says: 'The Home-maker should see there's breakfast enough to give the worker a good start for the day's work.' . . . Better breakfasts are in order!"

Victory before everything was the order of the day. As 20 million patriots produced in their gardens 40 percent of the nation's vegetables, Betty was posted in her test kitchen. One of her most valuable wartime contributions was "Your Share: How to Prepare Appetizing, Healthful Meals with Foods Available Today," a booklet distributed at General Mills' expense to almost 7 million Americans. Between its red, white, and blue covers were 52 menus, 226 recipes, and 369 tips for wartime food buying, preparation, meal planning, serving, entertaining, and etiquette.

Betty Crocker began her foreword to "Your Share" with a call to arms: "Hail to the women of America!" Her words enlisted an army of women:

> *Every American home-maker who selects food wisely, prepares it carefully and conserves it diligently is an important link in our national war effort. . . . At the end of the day, let us be sure we can say:*
>   *"I worked for freedom today.*
>   *I served at least one food from each of the basic seven food groups.*

   93

I prepared the food I served with care. I wasted no food this day."

Betty outlined the finer points of the Victory Lunch Box Meal: "Hearty, wholesome meal that combats fatigue, maintains efficiency on the job, interesting and appetizing, varied daily . . . Take a peek before you close the cover. Would you want to eat the contents 5 hours later?" Patriotic recipes, such as Service Cake, Victory Icing, Yankee Doodle Macaroni, Victory Pancakes, and American Chop Suey, filled Betty's wartime publications. When it came to wartime baking, "you can have your cake and eat it, too. . . . [M]ake smaller cakes. Use ½ or ⅓ of recipe. Make cup cakes. Serve uniced." Wedding refreshments for wartime included simple recipes for angel food or two-layer white butter cake topped with "an attractive flower decoration."

Another General Mills wartime booklet, "Betty Crocker's Thru Highway of Good Nutrition," won accolades from the American Red Cross for outstanding national service. The recipes in this booklet were informed by new government standards on vitamins and nutrition. By late 1942, the American Medical Association advocated the fortification of milk and flour. In October of that year, General Mills began identifying its "Kitchen-tested" Gold Medal Flour as "Vitamin-Mineral Enriched." The two added B vitamins and iron allowed the product to carry the AMA label of "preferred" food.

Betty's booklets, with their emphasis on a balanced diet of vitamin- and mineral-rich foods such as vegetables, milk, fortified bread, and lean meat, were often adopted for home economics curriculums. "The spotlight is on wholesome foods today!" Betty declared in September 1942. And Gold Medal Flour was a chart topper. "Give them this 'Vitamin Snack' when they're

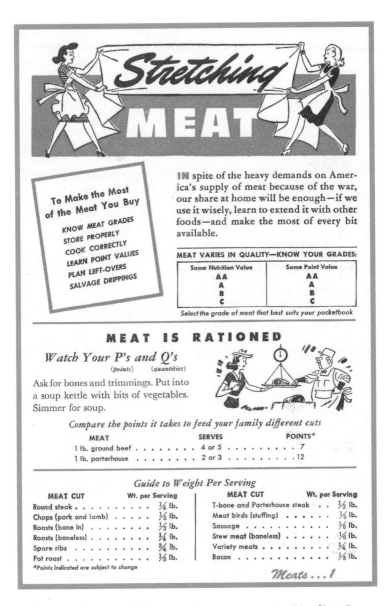

Stretching MEAT

To Make the Most of the Meat You Buy

KNOW MEAT GRADES
STORE PROPERLY
COOK CORRECTLY
LEARN POINT VALUES
PLAN LEFT-OVERS
SALVAGE DRIPPINGS

IN spite of the heavy demands on America's supply of meat because of the war, our share at home will be enough—if we use it wisely, learn to extend it with other foods—and make the most of every bit available.

MEAT VARIES IN QUALITY—KNOW YOUR GRADES:

Same Nutrition Value	Same Point Value
AA	AA
A	A
B	B
C	C

Select the grade of meat that best suits your pocketbook

MEAT IS RATIONED

Watch Your P's and Q's
(points)   (quantities)

Ask for bones and trimmings. Put into a soup kettle with bits of vegetables. Simmer for soup.

Compare the points it takes to feed your family different cuts

MEAT	SERVES	POINTS*
1 lb. ground beef	4 or 5	7
1 lb. porterhouse	2 or 3	12

Guide to Weight Per Serving

MEAT CUT	Wt. per Serving	MEAT CUT	Wt. per Serving
Round steak	¼ lb.	T-bone and Porterhouse steak	½ lb.
Chops (pork and lamb)	⅓ lb.	Meat birds (stuffing)	⅓ lb.
Roasts (bone in)	⅓ lb.	Sausage	⅙ lb.
Roasts (boneless)	¼ lb.	Stew meat (boneless)	⅙ lb.
Spare ribs	¾ lb.	Variety meats	¼ lb.
Pot roast	⅓ lb.	Bacon	⅛ lb.

*Points indicated are subject to change

Meats...1

From Betty Crocker's 1943 ration recipe and menu booklet "Your Share."

   95

Spare the Sweets

HERE'S THE WAY WE SAVE OUR SUGAR
WHEN WE MUST

S alt brings out sweet flavor of fruits and cooked foods. Add a pinch.
U se BISQUICK for shortcakes, fruit rolls, cobblers. It contains sugar.
G et prepared milk powders. No sugar is needed.
A fter dinner, serve jam with cheese and crackers.
R educe tartness of sour fruits by combining with dried fruits.

S erve fruits and vegetables naturally rich in sugar.
A dd sugar last when cooking dried fruits. Takes less.
V ary cereals with brown sugar, honey, syrup, dried and sweet fruits.
I nclude tapioca in fruit pies to cut tartness.
N ever throw away canned fruit syrup. Use for beverages, jellied salad, etc.
G et into the habit of serving coffee cakes and sweet rolls for dessert.

T horoughly dissolve sugar in beverages. Don't leave in bottom of cup.
I nstead of sugar, use corn syrup for beverages, fruits, sugar-water syrups.
P lan to serve desserts with no sugar (fruit cups, fruit gelatin, etc.).
S erve ripe fruits. They need little or no sugar.

Americans coped with wartime rationing of sugar and other foods with the

help of Betty Crocker's "Your Share."

         96

Stretch THE MILK SUPPLY

Nature's First Food

Nothing quite takes the place of milk—grownups need 2 cups a day—children need a quart.

Women and children first—if not enough for everyone, growing children have priority.

A complete protein—rich in calcium, some phosphorous and iron—with a good supply of riboflavin.

I've got Protein
I've got Minerals
I've got Calories
Who could ask for
anything more?

If You Don't Drink it, Eat it!

In mashed potatoes, cream soups, creamed vegetables, custards, ice creams, puddings, cheese, on cereals, etc. Milk is 13% solids. That's more solids than in some vegetables.

Save Fresh Fluid Milk

USE IT UP . . . Rinse cream bottles with milk, and use with milk; rinse milk bottles with water, and use in cooking. If milk sours, use it for waffles, pancakes, cookies, cakes, etc.

MAKE IT DO . . . Use top of milk for cream on cereals, in coffee, on desserts; use next milk for drinking,

and bottom of milk for cooking and baking. Use evaporated milk diluted with equal amounts of water for cooking and baking. And use dried milk, whole or skimmed, re-hydrated in 4 times the amount of water, for cooking and baking.

DO WITHOUT . . . Water may be used instead of milk in most bakings.

KEEP VERY COLD

Bacteria develops in milk 10 times faster at 55° than at 40°.

Take milk out of refrigerator just long enough to get needed amount. Return to coldest spot immediately. Keep tightly covered. Don't leave out on a sunny doorstep.

Low Temperature in Cooking, Too!

Cook milk mixtures in double-boiler. Bake milk dishes in slow oven *or* steam bake (in oven in pan of water).

Easy To Whip Plain Cream

Be sure to have cream, bowl and beater well chilled. Add ⅛ tsp. cream of tartar *or* ½ tsp. lemon juice to 1 cup cream. Whip with steady motion, increasing speed as cream begins to whip. (If cream is 1 day old, it should whip without adding other ingredients.) There are commercial products to make cream easy to whip.

12 . . . Milk

"Your Share" was distributed to almost 7 million Americans during World War II, free of charge.

   97

In 1941, Betty Crocker and several home defense agencies teamed up to create "Thru Highway to Good Nutrition," to help explain the importance of minerals and vitamins. This booklet received accolades from the American Red Cross.

hungry . . . milk and peanut butter cookies! made the Betty Crocker way." The milk-and-cookie snack, Betty explained, was a source of vitamins A, B$_1$, and B$_2$, and of calcium.

Up-to-date vitamin information was one feature of Betty Crocker's *War-Time Services for the Home-Front*, a series of guides to preserving the virtues of thrift and good housekeeping as a means of civil defense. "Every Homemaker a Captain in the Product Line Thru Home Conservation!" Betty Crocker declared by way of encouraging homemakers to take the Victory Pledge for home conservation. To be sparing in one's use of energy was paramount: heating the oven for a single dish or opening its door to peek at baked goods in progress counted as a vote for the enemy. With hearty fare sure to extend the powers of human endurance, true patriots prepared such ration-regulated meals as Short-Leave Dinner (included chicken-fried heart), Parachute-Landing Supper (baked squash stuffed with sausage), Mess Call Macaroni (platter of cooked macaroni with grated cheese), and Doughboy's Special (old-fashioned beef-vegetable stew).

Even in the darkest wartime hour, Betty remembered to celebrate. In December 1942, Betty wrote, "It will be a 'military' Christmas in millions of homes. And here's a 'military' idea for your Christmas baking." The recipe for "Military Christmas Cookies" was one of "the most practical the Betty Crocker staff has ever tested. One of the best-tasting too!" Betty provided traceable patterns for cookies in the shape of a pursuit plane, bomb, tank, shield, field gun, battleship, and sailor. The names of family members could be piped on with "No-Sugar Icing." Easy to make and inexpensive, the cookies could do double duty as Christmas tree decorations. And they were "just the thing to send away to that boy in the service!"

   99

Unlikely Hero

But Betty's holiday cheer could stretch only so far. Her loyal correspondents were frequently moved to confessions of despair. To be sure, the war ushered in a special brand of abysmal insecurity, as women reeled not only from the shock of a worldwide crisis, but from the very real possibility of losing their husbands, brothers, sisters, sons, and daughters. Wartime letters to Betty Crocker numbered in the thousands daily. Some contained devastating accounts of loved ones missing in action. Others simply asked what citizens could do to help win the war. Women often hoped Betty would take a special interest in news of their sons' successful flying missions, medals, or impending return from combat. Betty replied to each and every note with sympathetic encouragement and a congratulatory comment on the strength of American women. To a woman whose son and husband were both serving, Betty wrote:

> *Millions of us are praying for this awful war to end so all these young people serving their country so unselfishly may come home to peace and happiness. And I understand, too, how much you and your husband long to return to your little Cape Cod house on the coast of Maine! But how wonderful that he could serve his country again in this time of need! You and your loved ones have had a big part of this "war to end all wars!"*
>
> > *Cordially,*
> > *Betty Crocker*

Many of the wartime letters sent to Betty echoed the concerns of millions of women trying to "do their part."

In regard to Home Defense, my idea is that we women should concentrate on the proper nutrition of our families. In this way we will have more strong bodies, sharp eyes and steady nerves. We should see to it that every American citizen is supplied with foods, well balanced and abundant. In this way we can help our nation greatly in meeting any emergency of Home Defense.

*

I feel that the home, church and schools must work together. In so doing, I find satisfaction and happiness. To me, this is more vital than being in an assembly line. This is my contribution for a better world.

*

I have nine children, four married and gone, five still at home, so housekeeping is my war job.

*

Teach us the best, most wholesome, least expensive foods and food values for individual health—and we'll show you how we homemakers can bend our wills and our hearts and our very best efforts to aid those we love—and the country we love will profit by it. We each want to help— many of us don't know how—if someone can give us the tools and teach us how to use them wisely, I know that every homemaker, however inglorious her position may seem by comparison, will be the power by which all else moves and has its being.

*

I'm so sorry that I can't listen to your program any more Betty Crocker, I got myself a job in a defense plant to help end this thing.

The Betty Crocker Home Legion

The richer the dialogue between American women and Betty Crocker, the more convinced Marjorie Husted became of the need for proper recognition of homemaking. Husted believed every woman was essentially a homemaker, regardless of whether she held a paying job, because the brunt of the cooking and housework was hers to bear. With the strength of millions of letters behind her, in 1944 Husted created the Betty Crocker American Home Legion Program. Over the radio, Betty Crocker proclaimed the Legion's mission statement, and solicited enrollment:

> BETTY CROCKER   I do hope you'll take the time to let me know how you feel about my idea of banding together in a Home Legion to see that more recognition is given to homemakers for their contribution in the world. I can't tell you what an inspiration it is to me to get letters such as this, from a friend in Jasper, Indiana:
>
> WOMAN'S VOICE   . . . What these women need is to have their lives glorified—into the glamorous thing it is. If a woman is staying home with her children instead of going off to work in a war plant, she [too] is making a very important contribution to her country and should be told so. If she succeeds in rearing her children in a real home with a loving mother who is always willing to share her time with her children, she is surely going deeper into the real joys of life than the woman who must park her family on someone else to rear. Please keep up the good work of glorifying the home!

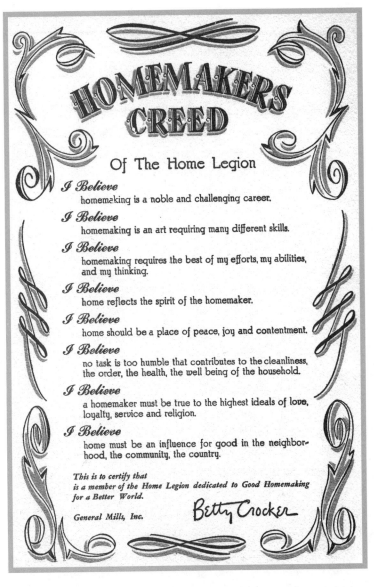

HOMEMAKERS CREED

Of The Home Legion

I Believe
homemaking is a noble and challenging career.

I Believe
homemaking is an art requiring many different skills.

I Believe
homemaking requires the best of my efforts, my abilities, and my thinking.

I Believe
home reflects the spirit of the homemaker.

I Believe
home should be a place of peace, joy and contentment.

I Believe
no task is too humble that contributes to the cleanliness, the order, the health, the well being of the household.

I Believe
a homemaker must be true to the highest ideals of love, loyalty, service and religion.

I Believe
home must be an influence for good in the neighborhood, the community, the country.

This is to certify that
is a member of the Home Legion dedicated to Good Homemaking for a Better World.

General Mills, Inc.

Betty Crocker

Seventy thousand Betty Crocker American Home Legion members received a copy of the Homemakers Creed, suitable for framing.

   103

BETTY CROCKER   Now perhaps some of you may have suggestions as to how we can all work together to glorify home life and to show the importance of homemaking. . . . Industry has developed a system of recognition for men. And men have the stimulus of competition with others doing the same type of thing they're doing. But women in their own homes usually are working alone without that sort of stimulus—without the recognition of having salary raises or having the boss tell them they've done a good job—and without being cited as an example to others. . . . And during the war years, you women have been doing *double*. Farm women have been taking the place of one or more hired men to produce the food to win the war. City women have gone into war plants and taken over war activities all along the line to help hold the *home front safe* and secure until our boys return. And in addition, most of these women are carrying on home duties too, working long hard hours to cover them all.

To further the cause of women's much-deserved recognition and moral support, Betty counted on listener feedback via written registration. There was no charge to join. Once registered, Betty invited each woman to complete a homemaking questionnaire detailing the goals Betty laid out on air. Legionnaires were eligible for prizes such as war bonds, and all received a copy of the Betty Crocker Homemaker's Creed (suitable for framing, of course).

The Homemakers Creed scroll does a lot for my home front morale. Whenever I glance at it, it reminds me of my duty

    104

to my home, my family and myself. I am a homemaker and proud of it. In fact, my Homemakers Scroll means more to me than my Bachelor and Master of Arts sheepskins.

*

I want to thank you for the Homemaker's Creed. I think it is so nice and means so much to me. I never realized home could be such a heavenly place until I heard your program. It really has done wonders for me and I love it. You must be a grand person.

The Betty Crocker American Home Legion Program inspired cultlike devotion, its ranks swelling to more than 700,000 women. Legionnaires and prospective members readily shared some of their most private thoughts with Betty:

Betty Crocker, I feel the need for the Home Legion very keenly—since through an unhappy atmosphere, and poor cooking, I lost my husband to another woman.

*

I think I also have been more interested in my home since I have joined your Home Legion. It has given me a little thrill inside to know that I could join such a club.

*

This letter is going to be filled with headaches but if I tell you just how it is, I think (I hope) you will be able to help me. To begin with, I am one of the poorest housekeepers there is. I have two children, and I never have any time for them. I'm short-tempered with them too. In fact, I never have time for anything. I can cook enough to get by, but

that is all. It never looks nice, and no one seems to enjoy it. It seems I'm always working, but the house is always a mess. I know I'm dumping a big load in your lap. But I do wish you could help me. Please send me anything you have that will get me straightened out. No one can blame my husband for being disgusted—I don't. That is why I want and need your help.

*

I was one who was beginning to believe that I had missed my calling so to speak, in the round of everyday homemaking. Thanks so much for the lift your Home Legion has already given me.

*

I'm very much interested in your Home Legion project and sincerely hope you can accomplish wonders with the average homemaker. Your Home Legion has given me real encouragement in my work.

*

Dear Miss Crocker, may I add my two cents, so the saying goes, about your Home Legion? The service you are giving housewives is marvelous. I must say you boost my morale 100% whenever I hear you.

In Betty's world, Mom and homemade apple pie were heralded as American treasures worth fighting for. The celebration of homemaking is often interpreted as reinforcing the role as women's best—and preferably only—aspiration. Yet, Betty Crocker's messages were never quite that simplistic. In the words of one letter writer, the Home Legion Program was "the finest thing that had ever been done for the American homemaker." For Betty's ever growing staff of career-minded women,

   106

this accolade was not a stopping point, but rather a challenge—to assess homemaking's precarious place on the edge of societal consciousness, to address the needs and the concerns of every kind of "working woman."

Keeping the Home Fires Burning

In 1945, the Office of War Information (OWI) enlisted Betty as the daily host of *Our Nation's Rations* on NBC radio. This four-month noncommercial venture explored home defense, the purchase of war bonds, Red Cross blood drives, consumer conservation, and other common home-front topics. Betty Crocker interviewed soldiers, civic leaders, nutrition experts, and government officials and their wives, and she updated listeners on worldwide food shortages and procedures for sending Christmas packages overseas. On March 14, 1945, the *Our Nation's Rations* broadcast began with the song: "Keep the Home Fires Burning."

ANNOUNCER Are Americans doing their part on the Home Front? What do you think? Betty Crocker thinks that the majority of them are—and she's here now to tell you why. As you know, she's one of America's best-known food authorities—so you can depend on her for some worthwhile suggestions that will help you make the most of your share of our nation's rations. She comes to you through the courtesy of National Broadcasting Company in cooperation with the Office of War Information. . . .

BETTY CROCKER When people are skeptical of whether American civilians are doing their part in the war—when

   107

someone asks a question as to how many women are really doing *their* share—I always wish they could see the letters from my radio friends, for *they* reveal how *many* know that *this is the time for greatness!* Older women are caring for their grandchildren while the mother does war work—younger women have gone into war plants and into the armed services. And *all* you homemakers have gardened for victory—and canned. And you've salvaged tin, and fats—and you have established meat stretching and sugar saving habits. You have saved and saved—and gone without. Upon you have fallen the brunt of these routines, daily, humdrum activities. They don't bring medals or parades with cheering crowds, but there is no greater patriotism—there is no truer greatness—than giving of yourself constantly, day after day, in these simple inglorious tasks. . . .

The Golden Era of Betty Crocker

The government placed its faith in Betty Crocker above all others to reach, educate, and influence American women and, to a larger extent, the entire nation. Betty was simultaneously accessible and untouchable. In war as well as in peace, her arsenal of helpful tips and recipes was unparalleled. Betty overshadowed other home service spokespersons, real or invented. But her vast achievements did not deter the competition from vying for a piece of Betty's pie.

Competitors were willing to pay top dollar for any successful approximation of the Betty mystique. During her Golden Era, would-be Bettys, each name safer-sounding and each face more homogeneous-looking than the last, paraded before Mrs. Con-

Postwar ad for Betty's labor-saving Pyequick.

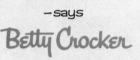

"TURN THE PAGE for my newest one-dish dinner

Dutch Pantry Pie!

Made with 4 famous products
from your pantry shelf!"

—says

Betty Crocker

OF GENERAL MILLS

A complete, meat-hearty
meal for six people —
economical, delicious!

Praised by our
Home Testers from
Coast to Coast!

Turn
page

Betty Crocker partnered with Wesson Oil, Spam, and Carnation Evaporated
Milk for this postwar Dutch Pantry Pie ad campaign.

   110

sumer. Martha Logan for Swift meats, Mary Alden for Quaker Enriched Flour, Jane Ashley for Karo Syrup and Linit Starch, Nancy Haven for Western Beet Sugar, Anne Marshall (later Carolyn Campbell) for Campbell Soup, Martha Meade for Sperry products, Mary Lynn Woods for Fleischmann's Yeast, Aunt Jenny for Spry Shortening, Mary Lee Taylor for PET Milk, Ann Page for A&P retail stores, Sue Swanson for Swanson's, Kay Kellogg for Kellogg Cereals, Virginia Roberts for Occident Flour, for General Mills' chief rival, Pillsbury Flour, Mary Ellis Ames (later Ann Pillsbury, though Ann never had a face)—competed for consumer dollars and brand loyalty.

These label ladies churned out recipe booklets, hosted homemaking radio shows, and answered consumer mail, just as Betty did. But lacking the cult of personality that surrounded Betty, her competitors faded into obscurity. As a brand icon in a class by herself, Betty Crocker had qualities—and secrets—her sisters could not buy or borrow, copy or steal.

Necessity is often credited as the mother of invention, but competition may be a close second. Betty's unprecedented success is responsible, in part, for launching the most famous baking contest in American history—the Pillsbury Bake-Off. According to an unpublished manuscript from one of the founders of Leo Burnett, a key advertising agency used by Pillsbury:

Now that all the new Pillsbury activity was in full flight, thoughts in 1949 began to turn to the bellwether of all Pillsbury products: Pillsbury's Best Flour. Although it had been in stores since Lincoln was President, it was strictly second fiddle to General Mills' Gold Medal Flour. Why was Gold Medal such a leading seller? Because it was backed by the claim "Kitchen-tested by Betty Crocker" and supported by

Martha Meade's

Failure-proof Recipes

The Betty-like Martha Meade for Sperry Flour.

112

Ann Pillsbury's
tasty talk

New...Brand New!
**Pillsbury
Pie Crust MIX**

One of Betty's fiercest competitors, Ann Pillsbury for Minneapolis-based Pillsbury flour, didn't even have a face.

   113

a constant stream of home service aids from Miss Crocker. This was one of the greatest concepts of all time and clearly indicated that you had to constantly help the housewife with recipe ideas and procedures if you expected to sell family flour. Furthermore, it meant that an entirely new form of home service had to be created if Pillsbury hoped to compete. . . . Instead of creating recipes (Betty Crocker) and supplying them to women, the process was reversed. The women created the recipes and sent them to us for the use of all women just like themselves.

In her newspaper column, Eleanor Roosevelt championed the Bake-Off as a "highly American" contest that "reaches far down into the lives of the housewives of America." Yet General Mills had news of its own. In its survey of homemakers conducted around the time of the Bake-Off debut, 44.3 percent of participants named Betty Crocker the "most helpful" home economics personality. Aunt Jenny, Betty's fiercest competition, came in a distant 5.6 percent, followed by the *Ladies' Home Journal* food editor, Ann Batchelder, at 4.1 percent. Ann Pillsbury rounded out the top four, at 2.7 percent.

America's First Lady of Food

The war years and the decade that followed were Betty Crocker's sweetest era. During the war, her mail volume shot up to 4,000 to 5,000 letters *daily.* By comparison, the popular radio personality Mary Margaret McBride received approximately 5,000 letters *weekly.*

Betty's visibility, or "impression" in marketing terms, shifted

Second best known woman

In 1945, *Fortune* magazine called Betty Crocker the second best known woman in America—second only to Eleanor Roosevelt. General Mills helped spread the word in a full-page ad.

from lifelike to larger-than-life. So extensive was her popularity that a wartime poll showed Betty Crocker was known in nine out of ten homes across the nation. And in 1945, *Fortune* magazine called Betty Crocker the second most popular woman in America, trailing behind only Eleanor Roosevelt. The piece went on to hail Betty affectionately as America's First Lady of Food.

As fond as *Fortune* seemed to be of Betty, in the glowing profile the publication had no qualms about delving into her quasi-secrets. The magazine publicly "outed" Betty, calling her "purely imaginary" and divulged her net worth: "$1 on the General Mills accounting books." The exposé might well have damaged Betty's pristine reputation—as her company must have been aware. But apparently they were confident that Betty's public cared more about her service than her true identity. As it happened, Betty's news didn't stop her adoring fans from buying her products, listening to her radio shows, and writing her letters.

Kitchen Dystopia

As peacetime came, Betty Crocker had her own cause for celebration: nearly a quarter-century spent with Mrs. American Homemaker. As the thrifty rationing of the war years gave way to postwar consumerism, General Mills called on her to rally the troops anew. Selling Mrs. Consumer was the task of the day, and Betty's work was cut out for her. The latest ideal had American women setting up housekeeping with ex-G.I.'s in sprawling new suburbs, with the latest electrical appliances. Neighborhoods were pristine and middle-class. Well-adjusted children greeted Father as he arrived home from work, while Mother efficiently tended to the family in a starched dress, tidily coiffed hair, and high heels. Everyone was happy, or so it seemed.

In the era of postwar abundance, Betty Crocker's name increasingly appeared on prepackaged food items.

New favorite with youngsters: chocolate milk poured on cereal. Particularly good with **CHEERIOS**, the new ready-to-eat oat cereal which looks like tiny doughnuts, has a robust, slightly salty flavor which a lot of people seem to like.

WHEATIES, "Breakfast of Champions", blend happily with almost any fruit. With **KIX** (crunchy puffs of presweetened corn) serve sharper fruits—peaches, berries. All 3 of these good cereals are valuable for food-energy, protein, important B-vitamins and iron.

Breakfast should contribute at least a fourth of your daily diet. Modern cereal grain foods—enriched bread and toast, whole grain and restored cereals such as Wheaties, Kix and Cheerios—furnish high nutritive value at very low cost.

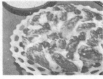

Gala French omelet: To serve 4, beat 6 eggs, add 6 tbsp. top milk, 6 drops Worcestershire Sauce, ¾ tsp. salt, dash pepper. Melt 3 tbsp. butter in skillet; add eggs and cook slowly just until eggs are set, lifting edges occasionally to let uncooked egg run under. When top is set, fold over. Serve with jelly.

MENU: Grapefruit; new handy Betty Crocker Cereal Tray of Wheaties, Kix, Cheerios; eggs; coffee cake; coffee, Vitamin D milk. Betty Crocker Cereal Tray: individual servings of Wheaties, malted whole wheat flakes; Cheerios, delicious new oat cereal; Kix puffed flakes of pre-sweetened corn; all ready-to-eat. Varied toppings: chocolate milk, fruit, brown sugar, honey, maple syrup

MORE FREEDOM ON SUNDAY

Betty Crocker of General Mills tackles the problem of mother's Sunday leisure...

Betty Crocker of General Mills

You've probably experienced the warm, proud feeling of sharing your favorite recipe with a friend or neighbor. It's the same kind of feeling Betty Crocker has when she passes along an idea that she and the Home Service Staff at General Mills have developed. For every time they perfect a new "Betty Crocker Recipe" or menu, they like to feel they are helping to make homemaking a little simpler and more pleasant for American women everywhere.

" I've often thought what a shame it is that the traditional day of rest is so often just another working day for mother. Of course, everybody likes special meals on Sunday, but with proper planning, I believe mother can have more time for recreation with the family and a chance to enjoy the real pleasures of homemaking.

For instance, on Sunday morning after mother prepares the fruit and coffee, assembles the "fixings," let everyone get his own breakfast. With three appealing cereals and a variety of toppings to choose from, coffeecake or toast and eggs any style, Sunday breakfast can be easy and happy as well as nutritionally sound. Somehow, even the smallest member of the family eats better when he can help himself." B.C.

Top all Sunday breakfast with a fragrant coffee ring from your favorite bake shop. Your baker and grocer offer a variety of coffee cakes and breakfast rolls made from finest home-type ingredients. Baked foods are low in cost, delicious, high in food value.

The glossy images of this era, epitomized by early black-and-white television shows like *Leave It to Beaver* and *The Adventures of Ozzie and Harriet,* come straight from central casting. Only a Norman Rockwell painting could be so selectively "perfect," especially when it came to the day-to-day lives of women. After the war, many working women were instructed to relinquish their jobs to veterans and resume their domestic stations. At the moment when patriotic pride easily trumped any impulse toward gender equality, women were left with little recourse than to enact what the editors of *House Beautiful* called the "biggest morale job in history" on their combat-weary husbands. Women's sudden loss of wartime independence bred disturbing new trends in depression and substance abuse.

As ever, letters to Betty Crocker articulated the prevailing misery of homebound women exiled in the kitchen wasteland. In 1963, Betty Friedan's groundbreaking *The Feminine Mystique* would call this affliction "the problem without a name." But even in 1946, Betty Crocker's Home Legion Program, with its themes of scarcity and making do, was fast becoming outmoded. That year Husted transformed the program into "Designs for Happiness."

Take pride in your homemaking skills, take time for yourself, take an interest in your husband's work, and take up a hobby topped Betty's cures for the ailing spirit of America's homemakers. According to her pamphlet "Better Home Management for Happiness":

Too many of these young homemakers of today find that they are absolutely unprepared for their new career. They reveal that if the home manager does not feel adequate to her job she cannot be completely happy. A successful home

is a structure of happiness. It is built day by day from daily activities—with hands, heart and mind. It needs a constructive plan—a design—to become a place of peace, joy and contentment.

Betty Crocker cited five keys to happiness: love and affection, good food, self-expression, pleasant surroundings, and spiritual faith. "Include them in your life's pattern . . . and you will build a true and lasting happiness for yourself and your dear ones." Betty also quoted letters from Home Legion members about the joy they found in homemaking:

I always try to have the children clean, my house a shining palace, and myself as radiant as possible when my husband comes home at night.

*

I keep a full cookie jar to treat the children's friends.

*

My kitchen radio has made it possible for me to enjoy many a grand opera while baking breads and pies and cookies.

*

I was blue until I decided that the most important thing for me was to do things that would please my husband. I leave undone unimportant work to have more time to improve my appearance. I cook dishes my husband likes best. I get someone to tend the store one day a week so my husband and I can go out for dinner. What a difference.

*

When I wash dishes, I see jewels in the soap bubbles in the dishpan.

*

  120

*I save countless steps by keeping a small towel over my left
shoulder while working in the kitchen. Many guests have
copied this habit of mine.*

During a 1946 winter broadcast entitled "Betty Crocker
Helps," Betty quoted a letter from a legionnaire who had helped
a young couple cope with differences that arose over the wife
keeping her paying job after the war. Betty sensed a conflict between expectations and reality.

*We know that millions of men returning from service have
a new appreciation of home and a new image of happiness.
To them happiness means the simple, fundamental homey
thing that they hold so much dearer after months or years
far away. And can the girls they marry understand this
yearning? Many of them are pretty young and they haven't
had these same maturing experiences.*

Fantasies of domestic perfection screamed from the headlines
of women's magazines. "What Is Your Dream Girl Like?" the
Ladies' Home Journal asked servicemen in 1942. First prefer-
ence went to the "Domestic type, fond of cooking and children,"
while "Business ability and braininess run a mighty poor second
to a talent for cooking." A January 1946 Crisco advertisement be-
seeched, "Cakes and Pies and Real Home Fries . . . that's what a
G.I. dreams of! Lady—make his dreams come true!"

For some women, such dreams were a test of sanity. "Dear
Betty Crocker," wrote "Young Mother" on January 16, 1946:

*I listen to your program and I get so darn tired of hearing
women who have 4 or 5 children, say they still have time to*

   121

do this *and bake* that *besides getting through with most of their work every day without help.*

You may think I'm an old grouch and a pessimist, but I never get through. I'm always tired and mostly unhappy.

I have two children—one 6 in school, the other 16 months. If you or someone could please tell me just how these other women do it—what's their routine? I've got to get through or I'll go crazy, I know. I hope you don't mention my name over the radio.

I like to cook and bake but I can't seem to get things done—or get in the mood to bake. My husband is a teacher and he's always dressed up and out meeting people, but I feel in a rut—it's horrible.

Sincerely, "Young Mother"

P.S. We can never get anyone to care for the children, but don't you think he should be willing to watch them while I get out once in a while to a show or to visit someone?

Betty Crocker read the letter over the air and asked her listening audience for their counsel. Listeners responded with prolific advice, decribing their own lives and making their opinions known:

You asked your listening audience to help the homemaker whose letter you read. I felt that I must answer, hoping, yes, even saying a little prayer, that perhaps my words could aid this evidently unhappy woman. So I shall just write a letter within a letter.

  122

Dear Friend,

As a way of introduction I will state that I have been married for 5½ years. A source of much pride and joy is our eight-month-old baby boy. Ours is truly a happy home. . . . It always has and always will take two to make a successful marriage. We mutually agree to treat each other with all the courtesy and thoughtfulness that we would afford any guest in our home. Think it over carefully, my friend. In my mind much of the "secret" of a happy marriage is contained in that one thought.

*

Let me remind you and the young mother that God has bestowed upon women the greatest honor that can come to anyone in this world. (That of bringing a life in this world: motherhood.) Next in line of first honor comes to a woman, (Homemaking) the highest calling a woman can have. Some man has chosen her of all women in the world to come and make a home for him. If women would only try and realize their place in life as a woman and quit trying to wear the pants and getting out and doing a man's work, there would not be as many broken homes and divorces. . . .

Let the young mother read my letter. Think of your work, my dear, as part of the bargain, see how well you can do it. Married life is the most competitive business in the world; you have got your man but it is up to you to keep him if you love him and want him. Stay neat, clean and interesting to him, stay his sweetheart—just because you are married, there is no reason why you should not still be the best of sweethearts.

In a May 14, 1949, ceremony in Washington, D.C., President Harry S. Truman and Bess Truman presented Marjorie Husted *(far left)* with the Women's Press Club award for her achievement in business. Other honorees include *(from left to right):* Dorothy McCullough Lee for government, Madeline Carroll for theater, Anna Mary Robertson (Grandma Moses) for art, Eleanor Roosevelt for Woman of the Year, and Mary Jane Ward for mental health.

Betty Crocker's staff replied by mail, suggesting that the "young mother" see a doctor, take time out for herself, accept her husband for who he was, and concentrate on raising her children. Betty also broadcasted the highlights from the letters she received. The "young mother" sent a thank-you letter back:

Dear Betty Crocker,
First of all I wish to thank you sincerely for all your kindness and help, and all your friends for the wonderful suggestions and ideas they so unselfishly offered. After hearing all the wonderful things other people have done in harder circumstances than mine, I feel quite ashamed of myself. But, so help me, I hope to the best of my ability to do all I can from here on out to make my home an ideal place to live and bring up children with happy memories of their childhood when they are grown . . . thank you again and to all your listeners I am grateful for their interest. Now if I can only prove myself worthy.

From 1924 to 1950, Husted's personal philosophies and Betty Crocker's corporate philosophies were almost indistinguishable. Through Betty, Husted told women what she believed they wanted to hear, given their circumstances, and at the same time she advocated empowerment to change their lives. With her briefcase full of letters that needed special replies, Husted took good corporate citizenship quite seriously. Thus Betty and Husted shared the spotlight on two noteworthy occasions. In 1949, Husted was named Advertising Woman of the Year by the Advertising Federation of America. The previous year, President Harry S. Truman presented Husted as a Women's National Press Club Woman of the Year, alongside fellow honorees Eleanor

Roosevelt and Grandma Moses. Husted also served as a consultant to the U.S. Department of Agriculture in 1948. Long after Husted retired, she was interviewed about her influence over Betty Crocker's persona for *Twin Cities* magazine:

> *It is very interesting to me to look back now and realize how concerned I was about the welfare of women as homemakers and their feelings of self-respect. Women needed a champion. Here were millions of them staying at home alone, doing a job with children, cooking, cleaning on minimal budgets—the whole depressing mess of it. They needed someone to remind them that they had value.*

The problem without a name would not be solved on Betty's watch. American homemakers' rampant discontent was beyond the jurisdiction of Husted or any flour company. Betty Crocker's Home Legion Program, "Designs for Happiness," like other special homemaker-recognition initiatives and radio programs, ran its course, peaked and bottomed out by the mid-1950s. Such ideologically based programs no longer seemed viable in a marketplace driven by rampant consumerism. What General Mills had to offer instead were new product lines designed to enhance the kitchen experience.

Chapter Four

Bake Someone Happy

Snickerdoodles

Puff during baking but settle down and look sugary and crinkly.

1 cup soft shortening (part
  butter)

1½ cups sugar

2 eggs

2¾ cups *sifted* GOLD MEDAL
  Flour

2 tsp. cream of tartar

1 tsp. soda

2 tbsp. sugar

2 tsp. cinnamon

Heat oven to 400°. Mix shortening, the 1½ cups sugar and eggs thoroughly. Sift together flour, cream of tartar, soda, salt and stir in. Form dough into balls of size of walnuts. Roll in mixture of the tbsp. sugar and cinnamon. Place about 2" apart on ungreased baking sheet. Bake *8 to 10 min. Makes about 5 dozen.*

From *Gold Medal Jubilee, Select Recipes, 1880–1955:*
A treasury of favorite recipes modernized by Betty Crocker

In a "kitchen just like yours," Betty Crocker's staff devoted their days to creating "breads, pastries, cakes—everything." Over the decades, the best of these recipes made their way into kitchens across America and became family favorites, shared by millions. Requests mounted for a "cook book full of [Betty's] famous tested recipes," until, in 1942, General Mills happily introduced *Betty Crocker's Cook Book of All Purpose Baking*. This paperback cookbook, a compilation of 220 of Betty's most requested recipes for cakes, pies, cookies, desserts, and breads, was available by mail order for 25¢.

All Purpose Baking was an overture to an instant classic, *Betty Crocker's Picture Cook Book*, often called *Big Red* for its red-and-white "early American" cover design. *Big Red* is the culinary equivalent of a national sing-along. Snickerdoodles, Oatmeal Raisin Cookies, Chicken à la King, Spaghetti and Meatballs, Pigs in a Blanket, Meatloaf, Tuna–Potato Chip Casserole—our taste buds know these tunes. A perennial best-seller in its category since its 1950 release, *Big Red* is in its ninth edition and has sold more than 30 million copies.

Big Red was the culmination of a half-century of recipe collecting, development, and testing by Betty Crocker's home economists. The staff of forty-eight was well equipped to turn out recipe books and pamphlets, but a production on the grand scale of *Big Red* required immense resources and time—ten years of planning, and three painstaking years of project development. The effort also called for the total restructuring of the department. One of Washburn Crosby's original Gold Medal Home Service staff members, Janette Kelley, was appointed

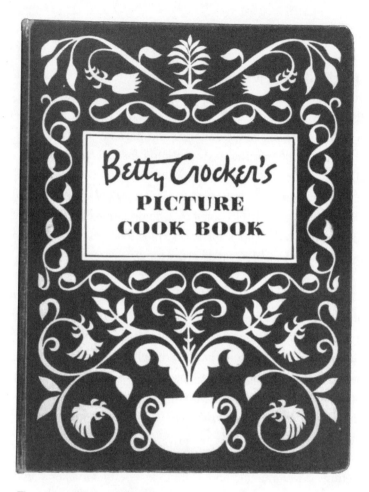

The original "Kitchen Bible," *Betty Crocker's Picture Cook Book* or, affectionately, *Big Red*, made cookbook history in 1950 when it debuted and shot straight up the best-seller charts.

   132

director of the Kitchens, as Marjorie Child Husted became cookbook editor-in-chief. The resulting assemblage of talent and expertise was primed to set the new standard for cookbook excellence.

The Cooking Bible

Consumers' first "glimpse" of the long-awaited *Big Red* came on the September 8, 1950, broadcast of *Betty Crocker Magazine of the Air.* For weeks, Betty and her sidekick, the announcer Win Elliot, teased audiences about "Betty's Mystery Gift," which, unbeknownst to listeners at home, had been strategically distributed to food industry tastemakers just before the publication date. On air, the book was presented to Sylvia Schur, the food and household editor of *Look* magazine.

> M.C.   Here you are! Now let's have that Grand Opening!
>
> SYLVIA   Stand back everybody! Here I go! . . . I'll bet I'm the envy of everybody who's received a mystery gift! Now I've got the ribbon off. . . . And here goes the paper! I'll open it up! And would you look at that! I wonder how many of you guessed that the mystery gift is *Betty Crocker's Picture Cook Book!*
>
> M.C.   That's what she said! It's what you gals have been asking for and waiting for years and years! *Betty Crocker's Picture Cook Book!* A Betty Crocker Cook Book with pictures . . . and lots of 'em in gorgeous color!

America's First Lady of Food appeared to have the postwar nation by the purse and apron strings as recipe-loving customers lined up in stores to purchase Betty Crocker's culinary masterpiece. A *Ladies' Home Journal* ad announced, "At last! A Betty Crocker Cook Book! Over $100,000 spent in testing and developing recipes before a single page was printed! Just off the press! Exciting, revolutionary, handsome! The result of 29 years' experience by the Betty Crocker Staff of General Mills, in food, cooking and homemaking." Betty's opus came in both loose-leaf ring binder with "deluxe" index tabs ($3.95) and case-bound ($2.95) editions. *Big Red* quickly became the gift of choice at bridal showers.

Within a year of publication, *Big Red* was a national bestseller, closing in on the Bible for the top spot. Though hundreds of cookbooks were on the market by 1950, just two could boast sales comparable to *Big Red*'s. *The Better Homes and Gardens Cook Book* was published in 1930 under the auspices of the Meredith Corporation's *Better Homes and Gardens* magazine— each 1930 subscriber received a complimentary copy—and went on to sell 15 million copies by 1996, when the updated eleventh edition was released. Irma S. Rombauer's *Joy of Cooking* was the leader in regular book-publishing channels. Originally self-published in 1931, the book became a best-seller for Bobbs-Merrill in 1943. Its 1951 edition, the closest contemporary to *Big Red*, sold 732,004 copies between 1951 and 1958.

Big Red enjoyed a distinct advantage over its competitors: the powerful marketing capacity of General Mills. The launch campaign was effective from the start, with *Big Red* drawing widespread media attention. The press was more than kind to Betty, touting her cookbook as essential for every homemaker:

> *This new cook book out-Crockers Betty Crocker. It is, in short, a dilly.* (HOUSTON POST)

   134

*

. . . if you haven't already asked for a mink stole, then ask for the new Betty Crocker's Picture Cook Book.
(ATLANTA CONSTITUTION)

*

. . . a cook book that has everything, plus the wonderful knowledge that every recipe will work—a cook book you'll always use for cooking, not just an ornament for a bookcase. (CHICAGO SUN-TIMES)

*

. . . probably the finest basic general cook book that has ever been published. (CHICAGO TRIBUNE)

*

. . . Betty Crocker's Picture Cook Book *is on its way to a sales record; initial printing of 950,000 copies is the largest ever, says McGraw-Hill distributor.* (NEW YORK WORLD-TELEGRAM SUN)

*

. . . one of the finest contributors to the advancement of the art of cooking that has rolled off the presses in many a year. (PITTSBURGH POST-GAZETTE)

*

. . . the new Betty Crocker Cook Book is going through the stores at the rate of 18,000 a week. Not bad when you consider that Hemingway, who is at the top of the best seller list, is doing about 3,500. (THE NEW YORK TIMES)

A 1955 celebration of Gold Medal's diamond jubilee trumpeted *Big Red's* bestsellerdom as a highlight of Betty Crocker's galaxy of stellar achievements.

   135

A Dream Come True

Betty's star power was housed in her famous test kitchens. *Big Red* invited readers in for a closer look. A "personal" letter from Betty welcomed cooks everywhere into her place of dreams.

> *Dear Friend,*
> *This book seems like a dream come true for us. And we hope it will be for the thousands of you who have requested a cookbook full of our famous tested recipes! And to those who have asked for a successor to that old brown-covered Gold Medal Cook Book which their mothers and grand-mothers treasured—here it is at last, a new and different cook book for a new age! . . . We hope this book will bring you more fun in cooking and a deeper joy in your home-making.*
>
> Betty Crocker

Light and lyrical text, cheery tinted line art, and personal hospitality—"Miss Esoline Beauregard of Fort Lauderdale, Florida said, 'Please try my mother's recipe' for French Breakfast Puffs"—weave through 16 chapters, 2,161 recipes, 633 instructional photo essays, 36 full-page color photographs, 20 sectional tabs, a glossary of cooking terms, an index, and tips for meal planning, table service, and shortcuts.

Big Red's most innovative feature was its pictorial, step-by-step directions; no other basic cookbook had such functional visual appeal. Hundreds of photographic close-ups—of hands mixing, blending, sprinkling, and kneading—illustrate Betty's tutorial, basic enough for a beginner, sufficiently sophisticated to satisfy a more experienced cook. Designed for adaptation ac-

The love/food combination was a popular theme in Betty Crocker's world.

cording to skill and desire, many "key" recipes begin with a foundation for more complex variations—a basic stew becomes Lamb Printanière, for example.

Even more magnificent than the key recipes were those that had earned the Betty Crocker star. "Don't miss the recipes marked with a ☆!" Betty coaxed. "They are special favorites with our Staff, and are served often in our own homes." And "Favorite" was hardly a casual term thrown around Betty's kitchens. A 1943 recipe for Golden Cottage Pudding—"We call it our vitamin dessert"—not only survived Betty's rigorous triple test, but had a successful run in women's magazines, finally earning its star. "Surprise! Guess what's in it! Moist, goozly!" ran *Big Red*'s plug for the dessert's secret ingredient, carrots.

Big Red's palate is decidedly all-American, with some foreign influences. Not until the 1980s would Betty begin to diversify with Chinese, Indian, "International," and Mexican cookbooks. For the benefit of the bottom line, General Mills' Gold Medal Flour and Softasilk Cake Flour anchor Betty's ingredient lists for a sublime array of breads, cakes, frosting, cookies, pies, and other desserts. Cake options run the gamut from simple "butter" cakes to Pink Azalea Cake; Lord, Lady, and Baby Baltimore Cakes; Cherry Angel Food Cake; Brown-Eyed Susan Cake; Red Devil's Food Cake; Creole Devil's Food Cake; and Peppermint Chip Chiffon, to name just a few.

These recipes were the subject of *Big Red*'s penultimate chapter, "Cakes," which bestows an honorific on homemakers one and all, provided they agree to follow Betty's directions: "We now proclaim you a member of the Society of Cake Artists! And do hereby vest in you all the skills, knowledge, and secrets of the 'gentle art' of cake making." Betty's lesson plan centered on a side-by-side pictorial comparison of the "good old way to mix a 'butter' cake"—the creaming method—with the new "Double-Quick" method—a one-bowl process introduced by Betty Crocker in 1944. Both methods were acceptable, though the creaming method is presented as "conventional" while Double-Quick is the "modern way." Either could be used to make Old-fashioned Yellow Cakes, Spice Cakes, Cocoa Cakes ("Dusky beauties you'll like"), Simple Sponge Cakes, Cream Cakes, Fruit Cakes, Specialty Cakes of Distinction, Chocolate Cakes ("For the man who comes to dinner . . ."), Egg Yolk Cakes, Wedding Cakes, Angel Food Cake, and Chiffon Cake. "Little boys from eight to eighty go for" Betty's Prize Fudge Cake. Some of Betty's cakes were not even of this world. "Have you ever seen a pale pink or delicate green angel?" she introduced her Peppermint Angel Food. "Well, we have."

So abundant were Betty Crocker's cake recipes that a single chapter could not contain them all. "Desserts" showcases tempting recipes for "Elegant Cake Desserts" and "Spectacular Cake Desserts" among the tortes, soufflés, pudding, ice cream, and fruit desserts.

The icing on the cake was a chapter of recipes for frostings and fillings—uncooked as well as cooked. Twisting the tip of a spoon created a decorative "hobnail" or swirl effect. If Betty's recipes for White Mountain, Lemon, Light Chocolate, Marshmallow, Comfort, Pineapple, Tutti-Frutti, or Satiny Beige frosting became too sugary, "All you have to do is beat in a little lemon juice."

"A butter icing is like a favorite cotton dress . . . simple and easy to put on . . . cooked white frostings like a perky street ensemble . . . and the extra touches for tinted coconut, toasted nuts, or allegretti are the gay accessories that make a costume special." Each of the twelve months of birthday cakes were dressed up in distinctive fashion.

What month is your birth date?
What star shines on you?
Here are jewels and flowers
And birthday cakes, too!

January birthday cakes call for white frosting with moist snowy coconut sprinkled on top and embellished with fresh red carnations. For May birthdays, frost the cake with tiny bouquets of Lilies of the Valley with an emerald green ribbon. And for July, "Tie up little bunches of sweet peas with satin ribbon. Place around cake and give to women guests."

A "Hallowe'en" cake with Peanut Butter Fudge Frosting is topped with melted chocolate in the shape of a witch. Father's Day is a time to establish family tradition—making Dad's favorite cake, with frosting of his choosing; "Present with a kiss hug." And any day is perfect for preparing Betty's Prize Fudge frosting, making sure to save the mixing bowl and spoon for the children to enjoy.

Friends of Betty

In the culinary tradition of giving credit where credit is due, Betty shares much of the recipe glory. Staff members and "friends of Betty," famous chefs, celebrities of the screen and airwaves, home recipe testers, and renowned hostesses, formed a dazzling array of contributors. *Big Red's* recipe for Crème Brûlée dishes up a rich historical context:

Served at a lovely luncheon by a delightful hostess, Elizabeth Case, co-author of "Cook's Away." This elegant dish was a feature of the famous hospitality of Thomas Jeffer-

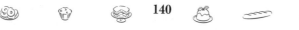

*son's Virginia home, "Monticello." He brought the recipe
from France in 1790.*

Eponymous recipes recall the folksy style of church cookbook
collaborations. Elena Zelayeta's Fresh Fruit Dessert is named
for the creator, "whose courageous spirit is an inspiration to us
all." A recipe for White Christmas Pie begins, "Pure white heavenly concoction created by Ruby Livedalen Peterson of our
staff . . . from an idea brought by Dixie Wilson of Mason City,
Iowa." A starred Egg Yolk Sponge Cake recipe is by one of
Betty's home recipe testers, Mrs. Ludwig Rice, a homemaker for
twenty-three years. And Betty's decadent Chocolate Joy Cake
recipe begins, "A family favorite from Mrs. Samuel C. Gale, wife
of our own Vice President."

Thoroughly upbeat, the cookbook periodically waxes outright
giddy. The recipes are punctuated by whimsical illustrations of
happy homemakers and their husbands, a cake frosting itself,
dancing peanuts, gleeful family picnics, pancakes in fancy
dresses, vegetables lifting weights, and grinning gingerbread
men. Betty's rhymes and sayings spring up all over, such as this
verse on egg freshness:

> Their shells should look dull . . .
> Not shiny or bright;
> But it makes no difference
> If they're brown or if they're white.

"Won't you come into our kitchen and join us in our 'Cooky
Shines'?" Betty asked. "That used to mean tea parties, but it's
what we call our sessions of cooky baking." *Big Red*'s "Cookies"
—based on "Betty Crocker's Picture Cooky Book," a 1948 recipe

Beau-Catchers (*and Husband-Keepers*)

Betty Crocker's Picture Cooky Book (1948) served as a prototype for *Big Red's* cookie section.

booklet that was revised, expanded, and, in 1963, published in hardcover as *Betty Crocker's Cooky Book*—was a primer on "saying it with cookies." Rolled, refrigerated, pressed, molded, and bar varieties were the secret to uniting friends and family, easing homesickness, celebrating Christmas, and creating life-long memories for the little ones. Every cookie imaginable is represented here, including such favorites as Chocolate Chip Cookies, Toffee-Nut Bars, Nut Sugar Cookies, and Chocolate-Frosted Brownies. Under the heading "Beau-Catchers (*and Husband-Keepers*)" appeared a recipe for His Mother's Oatmeal Cookies.

All You Have to Do

Big Red is not just for dessert. Every major recipe category—the proverbial soup to nuts—is fully represented, with dishes to suit every taste and occasion: Red Cinnamon Apples with Tiny Sausages, Melon Ball Salad, Braised Lamb Shank, Mushroom Polenta, Kaedjere, Lumberjack Macaroni, Hot Tamale Pie, Chicken Tetrazzini, Pompano en Papillote, Chicken Chow Mein, Cheese Dreams (grilled cheese sandwiches), Carrots Ambrosia, and Eggs à la Goldenrod. Betty's repertoire contains more than a few surprises. Nestled among menus for "cozy family suppers" are recipes for squirrel and rabbit dishes ("Best in the fall and early winter"), "Sub-Gum Curry," and Surprise Pancakes, subtitled "vegetables in disguise."

Big Red is just as much a reference work as it is a collection of recipes. Betty details her tips for cooking success down to the letter. "All You Have to Do" is her catch-phrase for ease and simplicity—whether the reader is learning to cook or looking for a refresher on how to properly store potatoes, slice bread, cut onions, or differentiate cuts of meat. The guide to "Useful Kitchen Utensils" compares gadgets from roasting pans to ramekins, and even the stickiest substances—from shortening to grated cheese—are a snap to measure Betty's way. Food substitutions, abbreviations common in recipe notation, nutrition, and meal planning all receive their due. "Smart homemakers say: 'My meals are more interesting . . . because I avoid repetition and plan for variety in color, texture, and flavor.'" Case in point is the perfection to be had in lattice-top fruit pies of every variety, equal in eye and appetite appeal.

Like Betty's radio shows, her cookbook is a compendium of food "facts" and historical tidbits. "Serve them up as table conversation," Betty suggested. "They'll make cooking, and eating, more fun." It was Cortez the Spanish conquistador, for instance, who initiated Westerners' love affair with chocolate, while appetizers date back to ancient Greece and Rome. Coffee's legacy from Abyssinia to the Americas is traced here. "Now the art of making good coffee is an asset to successful homemaking." And to accompany coffee—muffins, a term that comes from "little muffs" to warm the fingers. Hush puppies got their name from Florida hunters whose dogs whined over being denied the spoils of the camp fish fries. The hunters tossed leftover corn patties to the dogs, calling "Hush, puppies!" and they did.

The joy of cooking being far from a universal experience, Betty Crocker's staff modulated *Big Red* to suit the inhabitant of any kitchen, be she reluctant or passionate. Like any good book, however, it had to be read to be useful. "Heed the directions," readers were repeatedly urged. "Cooking success is up to you." Before she could do for others, a good cook had to care for herself. Saving time, energy, and money was an economy soothing to every spirit. In "Short Cuts" came a detailed blueprint for improving domestic life. True to the tenets of home economics, Betty advised homemakers to "Make every motion count" and "Let your head save your heels."

Living by these words enabled readers to avoid stressful days, saving labor by enlisting the family's help with chores or preparing and freezing large amounts of food. When circumstances called for "Special Helps," Betty suggested a few minutes' rest on the kitchen floor, harboring pleasant thoughts, pursuing a hobby, wearing comfortable shoes, alternating sitting and standing tasks, and taking time to notice "humorous" incidents, such as a kitten getting stuck in a tree, to narrate at dinnertime. These hints were relayed in an illustrated montage of blissful homemakers in dresses and frilly aprons. In cases of depression and fatigue, Betty prescribed proper rest, exercise, and sound nutrition. "Get a medical check-up and follow doctor's orders."

Cooks have long treasured *Big Red* for its usefulness, but history might value the book for something more. Its pages pinpoint the fundamental shift in American diets toward the factory-processed convenience foods that were becoming fixtures in the grocery aisles. For homemakers short on time and energy, Betty recommended all that supermarkets had to offer, proudly be-

Make work easy.

If you're tired from overwork,
Household chores you're bound to shirk.
Read these pointers tried and true
And discover what to do.

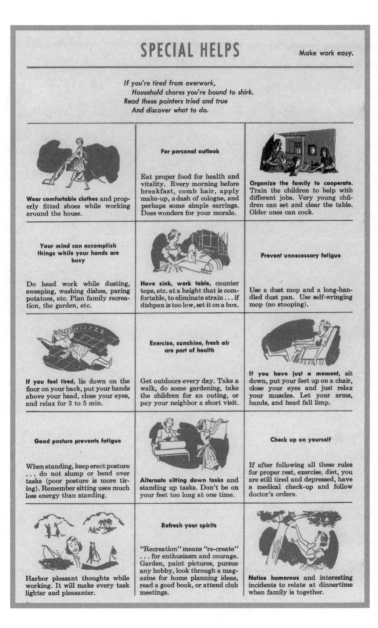

For personal outlook

Eat proper food for health and vitality. Every morning before breakfast, comb hair, apply make-up, a dash of cologne, and perhaps some simple earrings. Does wonders for your morale.

Wear comfortable clothes and properly fitted shoes while working around the house.

Organize the family to cooperate. Train the children to help with different jobs. Very young children can set and clear the table. Older ones can cook.

Your mind can accomplish things while your hands are busy

Do head work while dusting, sweeping, washing dishes, paring potatoes, etc. Plan family recreation, the garden, etc.

Have sink, work table, counter tops, etc. at a height that is comfortable, to eliminate strain . . . if dishpan is too low, set it on a box.

Prevent unnecessary fatigue

Use a dust mop and a long-handled dust pan. Use self-wringing mop (no stooping).

If you feel tired, lie down on the floor on your back, put your hands above your head, close your eyes, and relax for 3 to 5 min.

Exercise, sunshine, fresh air are part of health

Get outdoors every day. Take a walk, do some gardening, take the children for an outing, or pay your neighbor a short visit.

If you have just a moment, sit down, put your feet up on a chair, close your eyes and just relax your muscles. Let your arms, hands, and head fall limp.

Good posture prevents fatigue

When standing, keep erect posture . . . do not slump or bend over tasks (poor posture is more tiring). Remember sitting uses much less energy than standing.

Alternate sitting down tasks and standing up tasks. Don't be on your feet too long at one time.

Check up on yourself

If after following all these rules for proper rest, exercise, diet, you are still tired and depressed, have a medical check-up and follow doctor's orders.

Harbor pleasant thoughts while working. It will make every task lighter and pleasanter.

Refresh your spirits

"Recreation" means "re-create" . . . for enthusiasm and courage. Garden, paint pictures, pursue any hobby, look through a magazine for home planning ideas, read a good book, or attend club meetings.

Notice humorous and interesting incidents to relate at dinnertime when family is together.

A section in *Big Red* devoted to putting the joy in cooking.

Cake: *Betty Crocker Chocolate Devils Food Cake Mix.* Frosting: *new Betty Crocker Fluffy White Frosting Mix, with coconut.*

Kiss 'n' make up!

Who knows who began it? Who cares . . . really? The thing to do now is to end it. And our gal is making a valiant try. Steak . . . thick, no-respect-for-the-budget steak. And French fries. And a splendiferous, enormous, I-love-you-truly magic of a cake —a cake that whispers two words so potent he'll leap right out of his chair.

Can you count on that? Certain-sure. Just as sure as that someday they'll disagree again. This is a *family!* But they'll remember this night and the love that rings it 'round for a long, long two-hearts-forever time.

Of course you know how to get a cake that tastes and looks as great as that. This day . . . of all days . . . you make certain-sure to buy the mix that comes out perfect every time. It has Betty Crocker's name on the package. And you might want to bake it for the man you love . . . even if he didn't go away mad!

"I guarantee a perfect* cake—cake...after cake...after cake!"

Betty Crocker of General Mills

PERFECT: Yes, all our Betty Crocker Mixes—Cake, Frosting, Date Bars, Brownies, Pie Crust, Answer Cake—are guaranteed to come out perfect or send the box top to Betty Crocker, Box 200, Minneapolis, Minn., and General Mills will send your money back.

Betty Crocker encouraged women to "say it" with one of her cake mixes.

   146

stowing a special seal of approval on her own Bisquick, Crust-quick, soup, and cake mix products. "With [Bisquick] on the shelf, the busy homemaker, the modern business woman, or the impromptu hostess is prepared to meet any mealtime emergency with complete assurance and success."

Perfectly timed to usher in this brand-new era in American food, *Big Red* was, in Betty's words, "the happy ending we've anticipated from the very first." This culinary coup was no accident. By 1954, General Mills had invested over thirty years and more than $100 million in Betty Crocker; the success of *Big Red* generated a cookbook empire.

One after another, a legion of Betty Crocker cookbooks became instant best-sellers. Among her most memorable, especially for the Baby Boomer set: *Betty Crocker's Good and Easy Cookbook, Betty Crocker's Cookbook for Boys and Girls, Betty Crocker's Dinner for Two Cookbook,* and *Betty Crocker's Cooky Book.* When updated editions were ushered onto the market to reflect changing tastes and recipes, not everyone appreciated the favor, preferring instead to cling to their dog-eared originals. Repeatedly and for decades, consumers pined for the Betty Crocker they remembered from childhood. To the delight of millions, General Mills re-released the original *Betty Crocker Picture Cook Book* in 1998, *Betty Crocker's Cooky Book* in 2002, and *Betty Crocker's Cookbook for Boys and Girls* in 2003, reuniting cooks everywhere with the recipes that made Betty Crocker "the most trusted friend in the kitchen."

Chapter Five

*Just Add
Water!*

Chiffon Cake

The Chiffon Cake is the first new cake of the century—it's new in taste, new in texture and new in eating quality. Combining the best qualities of both angel food and butter cakes, it's also made an entirely new way.

2 cups *sifted* GOLD MEDAL Flour

1½ cups sugar

3 tsp. baking powder

1 tsp. salt

½ cup cooking (salad) oil

7 unbeaten egg yolks

¾ cup plus 2 tbsp. cold water

1 tsp. vanilla

2 tsp. grated lemon rind

1 cup egg whites

½ tsp. cream of tartar

Heat oven to 350°. Have ready ungreased oblong pan, 13 x 9 ½ x 2". Sift flour, sugar, baking powder, salt into bowl. Make a well and add oil, egg yolks, water, vanilla, grated rind. Beat with spoon until *smooth*. Measure egg whites and cream of tartar into *large* mixing bowl. Beat with electric mixer on high speed 3 to 5 min., or by hand until whites form *very stiff* peaks. DO NOT UNDERBEAT. A dry rubber scraper drawn through them leaves a clean path. Pour egg yolk mixture gradually over beaten whites—folding just until blended. DO NOT STIR. Pour into *ungreased* pan. Bake *45 to 50 min.*, or until top springs back

when *lightly* touched. Turn pan upside down, resting edges on 2 other pans. Let hang, free of table, until cold. Loosen from sides with spatula. Turn pan over and hit edge sharply on table to loosen.

From *Gold Medal Jubilee, Select Recipes, 1880–1955:*
A treasury of favorite recipes modernized by Betty Crocker

Dear Betty Crocker,
I derive so much help from your lessons. Before I started lis-
tening to your talks on WCCO, I made such wretched cakes
that my husband used to throw them down to the furnace to
burn them. But now I am really proud of the ones I make.

More than pies, cookies, bars, muffins, brownies, or biscuits, it
was cakes that topped Betty Crocker's recipe repertoire, like
thirteen-egg Angel Food Cake, the Calico Quilt Cake, Chocolate
Cream Cake, Strawberry Shortbread Cake, Marble Cake. Betty's
public could not get enough of them—and thanks to General
Mills' plentiful cake-centered advertising campaigns, there was
little risk of deprivation. Cake-naming contests, international
cake recipes, cake history tidbits, and newly developed cake
recipes—especially for chocolate cake—dominated radio broadcasts. Betty believed that every day was a good day for cake, but
some cakes were meant for special occasions. "Cakes have become the very symbol of home life in our country. From the beautiful cake for the announcement party—to the triumphantly
towering wedding cake—and children's birthday cakes, blazing
with candles—to the proud cake celebrating the silver or golden
wedding—cakes play an important role in the most significant
moments in our lives."

After wartime flour and sugar rationing were suspended, in
1946 and 1947 respectively, the remainder of the decade saw
more than a billion cakes made or bought yearly. Among the
highest—and most personal—forms of culinary achievement,

cakes were far more than sweetened bread. As Betty liked to say, "For any occasion, big or small, there's nothing like a home-baked cake to make the moment memorable."

Cake Magic

Betty Crocker's cake-baking heritage begins with her earliest days. In 1922, a full-page ad for Gold Medal Flour featured her recipe for Gold Medal Cake with chocolate icing. "There is something about a good cake all wrapped up in a coat of creamy chocolate frosting that makes people feel that your dinner has been a success," Betty rhapsodized. Desirous of the acceptance and approval Betty described, homemakers increasingly demanded specialized cake flour. Before the decade was out, General Mills had created the finely milled Gold Medal Special Cake Flour (later renamed Softasilk Cake Flour). In a 1930s radio broadcast, Betty Crocker announced the new arrival:

> *Many women have become so accustomed to using a special cake flour for part of their baking that they demand this type of flour occasionally. Our company has always aimed to give customers what they want to use, and we are therefore milling a special cake flour for the women who want it. . . . If you are one of the women who would like to use a cake flour occasionally when you want to make a special birthday cake or cake for a bridal supper, or one to enter in a cake contest at a food show or fair, I recommend that you try our Gold Medal Special Cake Flour.*

Betty's first all-cake recipe booklet, "New Party Cakes for All Occasions" (1931) opens with the illustrated saga of two young

154

From "Betty Crocker's How to Have the Most Fun with Cake Mixes."

brides making birthday cakes for their husbands. The first bride, a radio student of Betty Crocker, insists on using Gold Medal Cake Flour and a "Kitchen-tested" recipe. The second bride phones her grocer to send over any kind of cake flour. After mixing, baking, frosting, serving, and eating, the first dashing couple gaze happily into each other's eyes: "The Birthday Cake made this Gold Medal Way was a great success. It was so delicious that husband asked for another piece and said he had the most wonderful little wife ever. The perfect cake made it the perfect day." The second bride is in tears while her disgusted husband looks away. "The other bride's adventure in cooking didn't have such a happy ending. She had not used Gold Medal Cake Flour, and a Gold Medal recipe; and husband, poor chap couldn't even manage to eat a whole slice of her flat, heavy cake. And that spoiled the day for both of them!"

So that the low points of cake history would not be repeated, Betty devoted an entire 1935 broadcast, "Cake Clinics," to fixing "sick" cakes.

> *This morning I am going to talk about the food that strikes the highest note in the entire meal—the cake you serve for dessert. I think among all the foods served at your table, this is one where your reputation as a hostess and as a good provider for your family is most at stake.*

Betty's cures for ailing cakes included: avoiding packing in too much sugar into the measuring cup by spooning as opposed to scooping out of the bag; treating ingredients gently for best results; adding just enough—never too much—leavening; and sifting flour only once.

Emergency Cake was at the ready for impromptu entertain-

 156

ing, but sometimes it took a bit of extra effort to achieve a real party pleaser. Betty Crocker's Queen of Hearts Cake called for a doll to be inserted in the middle of the cake and "dressed" with an intricate frosting skirt. Pink frosting and red candy hearts could transform this pound cake into the ideal dessert for St. Valentine's Day or a bridal shower. As Betty's staff experimented throughout the years to perfect "quick and easy" cake batters, Queen of Hearts Cake was eventually streamlined into Doll Cake, popular at little girls' birthday parties.

Double-Quick

In 1944, Betty Crocker's staff discovered a new method for cake baking—Double-Quick, as it came to be known—a one-bowl process that cut prep time in half. In an October 1944 broadcast Betty celebrated twenty years on the radio with a recipe for Anniversary Cake:

> *It really is beautiful enough and delicious enough to grace any festive occasion. So maybe you'll want to plan a party around it. Invite your friends over for cake and coffee! And then just listen to the exclamations when you cut your cake and when they take their first bite! Then you can tell them that you made it by our new streamlined method—the quick, easy method of cake-making developed by our staff last year after months of experimenting. You know, this method is revolutionizing cake making all over our country. Everyone is talking about it! Wherever I go, visiting home economics departments of magazines—or in groups of home economists—at luncheon meetings, etc., someone*

   157

will say (with a glow), "I made one of your new method Softasilk Cakes the other day and really it was just superb!"

And, you know, the best of it all is that it's so easy! There's just one bowl to wash—one spoon for mixing (or your electronic mixer)—there's no longer creaming of the shortening and sugar—and no separate beating of egg whites and egg yolks. It really is streamlined—and all the guesswork is taken out of it!

Promotions for Double-Quick were deferred for the duration of the wartime flour ban. In 1946, Betty reintroduced Double-Quick via full-page magazine ad. "Good News! On the Betty Crocker Silver Anniversary America's favorite flour is again available . . . to bring you *carefree* baking days once more." Betty Crocker promised "4 Steps in 4 Minutes" for a delicious home-made cake: Sift flour, add ingredients, beat for two minutes, and beat in eggs for another two minutes.

An homage to Double-Quick emerged in the form of a twenty-two-minute 16mm color film to be screened for high school and college home economics classes, women's clubs, and youth groups: *400 Years in 4 Minutes*. It opens with the serving of a gigantic cake at a lavish banquet for King Henry VIII. The film quickly advances four centuries, culminating in a demonstration of Double-Quick in the 1945 Betty Crocker Test Kitchens.

Mystery Cake

Betty Crocker played a part in the notorious rise of one very ex-pensive cake—Chiffon, heralded as "the first new cake in 100 years!" Before 1948, cakes were traditionally classified as either butter or sponge (angel food belongs in the sponge category).

NO. 50 PLAIN   **20 VALUE**

THE CAKE DISCOVERY OF THE CENTURY

Betty Crocker
"*Chiffon!*"

An exciting new type of cake!

1. "It's more delicate than finest Angel Food (and more moist).
2. "It's as rich tasting as 'butter'-type cakes.
3. "It's easier, faster to make than ordinary cakes."

Betty Crocker of General Mills

BETTY CROCKER *Spicy "Chiffon"*

WARNING: Do not use any flour except Gold Medal with this recipe. The proportions might not be right with a different flour. Do not risk a food-wasting baking failure—use Gold Medal.

Harry Baker invented a new cake-baking technique and sold it to General Mills in 1948 for a large, undisclosed sum.

RECIPE for *Betty Crocker* "CHIFFON" CAKE

Betty Crocker
of
General Mills

Betty Crocker
explains:

"'Chiffon' is the 1st really NEW cake in 100 YEARS!"

More delicate than angel food . . . richer-tasting than "butter"-type cakes . . .
. . . easier to make than ordinary cakes!

A NEW TYPE CAKE—not angel food, not sponge cake—not butter or pound cake—the glamorous new Betty Crocker "Chiffon" Cakes combine the best points of each! They're totally new in taste—in texture—in the way they're made!

HIGH, LIGHT AND HANDSOME! This beauty cake is deliciously moist-tasting, keeps fresh amazingly long. Whether you make the large tube cake or smaller square cake (*recipes on back*) you'll be overjoyed at the praises you get! Such smooth velvety eating quality, delicacy, volume and feathery lightness have never been combined.

"BEGINNER-EASY"! Just follow three simple steps in the recipe. The liquid shortening—used in this recipe—will be a surprise to you. It makes the mixing easier. New Chiffon Cakes *rise as high as angel food* . . . yet take 5 less eggs!

TRY IT NOW! With Softasilk, the Betty Crocker Cake Flour, you're sure of success! It enables the delicate rising action of eggs and baking powder to reach full height—makes for finer texture. *Better get a package of Softasilk now!*

RECIPE IS ON THE BACK

Chiffon combined the richness of butter cake with the lightness of sponge cake.

But an aptly named cake baker, Harry Baker, from Hollywood, California, challenged conventional cake wisdom and started his own mini baking revolution.

Baker, originally an insurance salesman and recreational cook, enjoyed all cakes, but dreamed of combining the richness of butter cake with the lightness of sponge cake. So he set out to invent a new kind of cake. Baker's ambitious pursuit took years and produced about three hundred baking disasters; finally, in 1927, his efforts brought forth an upside-down cake that was described as light, tender, delicate, glamorous, and delicious, with sensational volume. Dessert lovers clamored for a taste, hoping to name Baker's reputed mystery ingredient.

Baker doggedly guarded his secret, fending off the interlopers who were constantly and unsuccessfully "volunteering" at his kitchen. As word of Baker's miracle cake spread throughout Hollywood, orders soared beyond his capacity to fill them, catapulting him to the rank of most sought-after cake baker on the Hollywood catering circuit. Both MGM and RKO granted screen time to his creations, and chiffon cake was added to the menu at the Brown Derby restaurant.

A cake fit for American royalty, Baker's confection was served to Eleanor Roosevelt while she was visiting Los Angeles. The First Lady asked Baker to instruct the White House cooking staff in his baking secrets, but Baker respectfully declined. Almost twenty years passed before Baker went public with the recipe, timing the sale of his secret to the lifting of wartime restrictions. After reading the *Fortune* magazine citation of Betty Crocker as the second most popular woman in America, he decided to pay her a visit.

Rumors of Baker's Hollywood mystery cake preceded him. Upon his arrival in Minneapolis, intrigued General Mills execu-

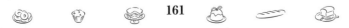

tives offered him free run of Betty's kitchens. But Baker preferred to bake nights and Sundays at the Minneapolis Gas Light Company Test Kitchens. Once samples of his cake had earned the Betty Crocker seal of approval, negotiations began. However, General Mills would not strike a deal until the secret ingredient was revealed. With that, Baker exposed his cake for what it was: flour, sugar, baking powder, salt, five egg yolks, a cup of egg whites, lemon rind, cream of tartar, and, instead of shortening— *cooking oil.*

While Baker contemplated what he would do with the large (undisclosed) sum, Betty's staffers got to work. Behind closed doors, General Mills' food chemists and home economists fine-tuned Baker's somewhat unstable recipe for eleven months. Finally, in 1948, the recipe for Betty Crocker's Orange Chiffon Cake debuted in *Better Homes and Gardens, Ladies' Home Journal,* and *McCall's.* The *Minneapolis Tribune* and others broke the news under the headline *Mystery Cake—Secret Ingredient X Revealed for Baking Mammoth Chiffon. Look* magazine and various home economics publications also covered the mystery cake story as curious bakers around the nation tried out this famous new recipe. More complex than the basic add-and-cream cake, the chiffon included the crucial step of folding in the eggs. Baker's addition of two leavenings, cream of tartar and baking powder, assured the rising of the cake, to the great delight of many home bakers.

General Mills conducted market research on the Chiffon Cake sensation and concluded it a success. Homemakers who baked the cake praised its simplicity as well as its pleasing texture:

Very fluffy and delicious. Very easy to make, too.

*

I think the cake is wonderful and has the right name—
Chiffon—very light and fluffy.

*

Cake was easily made, light in texture, nice flavor—deli-
cate as all sponges are supposed to be—moist and not a bit
dry as some are prone to be.

However, as one candid letter reveals, positive results were not
quite a given:

Dear Betty Crocker,
I am writing you because I'm confused. Right now I am in
the process of making your new "Miracle Cake" and be-
lieve me if it turns out, it will be a miracle! The Thing is in
the oven and I am waiting with bated breath.
. . . To explain, I have no 10-inch tube pan, four inches
deep, so The Thing is in two pans, one a loaf pan 8½ by 3½,
3 inches deep. The other is a regular 6-inch tube pan, 3½
inches deep. My oven has no control on it, being vintage
1924. I guess it is lucky to have a door, but I have
always used the by guess and by gosh method and have
been very fortunate with everything. But this Thing has me
scared. At the moment there is the most wonderful odor
filling the kitchen. I have just taken a peek and things are
happening, the batter is rising all over the place. I forgot to
explain that my young son broke the only good clock in the
house, so I am timing it by the General Mills Hour [on the
radio].
My question is this, can this wonder be made in any
other flavor than orange or lemon? My husband is one of
those men that likes any cake as long as it is chocolate cake,

163

*so although he will eat this or I will ram it down his throat,
I would like to know if you can make a chocolate version. . . .*

*Although I know as Betty Crocker you are not a real
person, believe me you will have either real curses or real
praise heaped on your soul depending on the outcome of
this venture. You can tell Mr. Baker that he never put his
discovery to the test I have put it through.*

*Thank you so much for helping me through this trying
period.*

*Sincerely yours in hope and desperation,
Name Withheld*

The anonymous letter writer soon got her wish, as Gold Medal
Flour recipe inserts and "Chiffon Cakes by Betty Crocker" circu-
lated chiffon recipes in a host of flavors: Coconut Chiffon, Spicy
Chiffon, Chocolate Chip Chiffon, Maple Pecan Chiffon, Royal
Hawaiian Chiffon, Banana Chiffon, Sunburst Chiffon, Burnt
Sugar Chiffon, Holiday Fruit Chiffon, Bit O' Walnut Chiffon,
Cocoa Chiffon, Peppermint Chip Chiffon, and Cherry Nut Chif-
fon. Like any fad, the popularity of chiffon cake did not endure.
Within fifteen years or so, Betty's public lost interest and Chiffon
quietly slipped away.

The Great Cake Mix Controversies

By 1952, the average U.S. grocery stocked 4,000 items, up from
approximately 870 in 1928. The old-fashioned way of food shopping, with consumers following the advice of their trusted
grocer, was giving way to a more direct interaction with the mar-

Betty Crocker was a triple threat in the burgeoning cake-mix market of the late 1940s.

   165

keting incentives of prefabricated food and brightly colored packaging that promised newness, ease, and convenience.

General Mills, firmly rooted in grain products—Gold Medal Flour, Bisquick, Softasilk, Wheaties, and Cheerios—embraced cake mixes, but Betty was a late arrival to the party. P. Duff and Sons, a molasses company, pioneered the "quick mix" field by marketing the first boxed cake mix in the late 1920s or early 1930s. Continental Mills, the Hills Brothers Company under the Dromedary label, Pillsbury, Occident, Ward Baking Company, and the Doughnut Corporation all produced versions of cake mixes before World War II. But problems of spoilage and packaging abounded, keeping mixes from widespread consumption and acceptance.

In November 1947, after four years of cake mix research and development, General Mills' test markets were exposed to the "Just Add Water and Mix!" campaign for Betty Crocker's Ginger Cake. After a final assurance from the corporate chemists that the boxed ingredients would indeed perform as advertised, the mix was made available for limited distribution on the West Coast. Within a year, it made a national debut that excluded the South (presumably, product testing there proved futile). While Ginger Cake required a nine-inch-square pan, designers projected that the PartyCake line, already in development, would offer home bakers a choice of using either two square pans or one 9-inch-by-13-inch rectangular pan, a size and shape that were becoming more popular.

As layer cakes were a uniquely American creation, they seemed a fitting choice for PartyCake, the next wave of Betty Crocker mixes. The layered butter PartyCake mixes—in Spice, Yellow, and White cake varieties—and Devils Food Cake Mix were priced at $.35 to $.37 per red-and-white box. "High impact"

Do try this new way to serve my good, rich Chocolate Devils Food

A 1953 ad for Betty Crocker's Devils Food Cake Mix. Many of Betty's loyal fans took offense at the word "devil" on her packaging.

colors were essential to enticing "the ladies who trundle their little shopping wagons among the shelves and tables" of the supermarket, wrote the prominent industrial designer Egmont Arens in 1950. Sophisticated "color studies" determined that women were especially drawn to red packages, like the ones that held Betty Crocker cake mixes, while men preferred blue.

Plenty of consumers saw red over the use of the word "devil" on cake mix packaging. Legend has it that individuals fearful of Satan worship implored Betty in writing to replace the word "devil" with something less evil-sounding. But the flour company would not budge, considering that "Devils Food" preceded Betty Crocker and was well known as a so-good-it-must-be-a-sin kind of cake. To this day, Devils Food remains one of Betty's most popular mixes.

The postwar quest for cake mix supremacy unfolded much like the flour wars of the 1920s. In 1948, Pillsbury was the first to introduce a chocolate cake mix. Duncan Hines stormed the market in 1951 with "Three Star Surprise Mix," a three-flavor wonder that in three weeks captured a 48 percent share. But Betty persevered, steadily rolling out a full range of flavors and varieties: Yellow (1952), White (1952), Honey Spice (1953), Angel Food (1953), Marble (1954), and Chocolate Malt (1955).

The very marketable premise behind cake mixes was, and still is, the ability to have a fresh "home-made" cake with very little time and effort. Though Betty Crocker—like her competitors—promised that cake mixes offered freshness, ease, and flavor in a box, the market was slow to mature. Puzzled, marketers reiterated the message that homemakers need only drop this scientific marvel into a bowl, add water, mix, and bake. But that was still a little *too* good to be true for Mrs. Consumer America. Certainly, cake mixes sold, but—compared with the early performance of Bisquick or Aunt Jemima pancake mix—not up to industry expectations.

The "quick mix" or "baking mix" industry, eager to correct the shortfall, conducted research even as the development of new mixes continued. General Mills considered the market research of the business psychologists Dr. Burleigh Gardner and Dr. Ernest Dichter to explain the mediocre sales of cake mixes. The problem, according to the psychologists, was eggs. Dichter, in particular, believed that powdered eggs, often used in cake mixes, should be left out, so women could add a few fresh eggs into the batter, giving them a sense of creative contribution. He believed, too, that baking a cake was an act of love on the woman's part; a cake mix that only needed water cheapened that love.

Whether the psychologists were right, or whether cakes made with fresh eggs simply taste better than cakes made with dried eggs, General Mills decided to play up the fact that Betty Crocker's cake mixes did not contain dried egg whites, egg yolks,

   168

Betty Crocker Cake Mixes bring you that Special Homemade Goodness

...BECAUSE YOU ADD THE EGGS YOURSELF

LIGHT, FLUFFY CAKES

They're made with famous Softasilk Cake Flour...and *you* add the eggs!

RICH, MOIST CAKES

They're made with the finest premium quality cake shortening...and you add the eggs!

TALL, LUSCIOUS CAKES

They're genuine Betty Crocker recipes, all measured and blended. You get a full pound and a quarter of cake mix in every package—and *you* add the eggs! No wonder 9 out of 10 women, in hundreds of tests, said that cakes made with Betty Crocker Cake Mixes and their own fresh eggs gave them *bigger, taller* cakes than the other cake mixes they tested.

PUT SUMMER SUNSHINE IN WINTER MEALS WITH
California Fiesta Cake

Just bake a big, moist, fluffy, fresh egg cake with Betty Crocker's new YELLOW Cake Mix. Fill, and top with whipped cream and sweet California canned Cling peaches. Quick, easy and oh so good.

Betty **Crocker**
Cake Mix
YELLOW
You add fresh eggs and water

Betty Crocker
CAKE MIXES

There are two kinds of cake mixes. This is the *only* nationally sold cake mix that lets you add the eggs—the only one that gives you that special homemade goodness.

Try All These Wonderful Betty Crocker Mixes   WHITE · YELLOW · DEVILS FOOD · GINGER BREAD

Some of Betty's competing cake mixes required no eggs, just the addition of water or milk.

   169

or dried eggs of any kind. (Betty's Ginger*Cake* was an anomaly because it didn't necessarily require eggs, powdered or otherwise.) Before long, cake mix started to gain some acceptance and notoriety; even Mamie Eisenhower instructed her cooking staff to use this novel invention at the White House. An "independent market organization" conducted research with hundreds of homemakers in Philadelphia, Cincinnati, and St. Paul, comparing Betty Crocker brand cake mixes with two other brands that used dried eggs in their cake mixes. Betty Crocker, once again, reigned supreme.

But despite surveys, First Lady endorsements, reformulated mixes, and rising sales, controversy over cake mix persisted. Eggs or no eggs, not everyone was content to slide down the slippery slope of the "modern way." Reducing to a powdery mix such an affectionate act as baking for one's family disturbed some long-time Betty Crocker fans. The very idea that she would endorse such a cheap, quick, and easy baking substitute flew in the face of everything they knew about wholesome, wise, and traditional Betty Crocker.

And even if women decided that cake mixes were fine in a pinch, would those who found cake mixes akin to shoddy, careless homemaking pass cruel judgment? Would cake-mix families compare unfavorably to those eating made-from-scratch cakes? Some husbands did not like the idea of their wives using boxed cake mix any better than than they did serving a store-bought cake. Cake mixes, like other convenience foods, were a risk that some homemakers were not willing to take.

Still, such trepidation did not stop cake mixes from steadily merging into mainstream popularity. From 1945 to 1951, consumers purchased 937 million pounds of cake mix; use of mixes increased 343 percent. Not everyone was proudly waving the proofs of purchase. Some took to using cake mixes in secret and passing off the results as their own creation. And incidents of clandestine cake mix use were not isolated! Busybodies excused themselves from parties just long enough to rifle through the kitchen trash can for empty cake mix boxes.

Still, Betty gave her friends permission to mix it up, inviting them along to the festivities: "Let's have a pink party . . . it's so easy with my White Cake Mix." And so it was. With her convincing command of the trendy cake mix market, Betty Crocker cast aside a few of her traditional trappings, tempting some holdouts to consider that using a mix from time to time was not altogether bad home economics.

From the late 1940s through the 1950s, Betty Crocker did her part to guide her loyal public through the lucrative transition from scratch to mix. Her catchy slogan, "I guarantee—A perfect cake every time you bake . . . cake . . . after cake . . . after cake," sang out from radio, magazine, and television advertisements for Colorvision Cake Mix (Just add your favorite fruit gelatin!), Angel Food Mix, Peanut Delight Mix, Orange Chiffon Cake Mix,

Inspired by the popularity of color television, Betty cross-advertised in magazines as well as appearing in CBS's first color television commercial.

and Marble Cake Mix, along with frosting mixes—Angel Fluff, Chocolate Fudge, Chocolate Malt, and Peanut Creme. Always one for keeping the lines of communication open, "Write me one of these days, why don't you?" Betty urged. "I'd love to hear how your family feels about my white cake (and have your tried our latest—Honey Spice Cake Mix?)."

During the early cake mix years, new products were frequently added to the rotation. In 1954, Betty Crocker targeted individuals and small families with Answer Cake, an all-in-one package of cake mix, aluminum foil baking pan, and frosting that could serve six to twelve, depending on the size of the slices. "Cake Mix Magic" and "How to Have the Most Fun with Cake Mixes" instructed consumers on the versatility of mixes, which could be adapted to Betty's most popular cake recipes. Long-standing favorites like Baked Alaska, Coconut Cream Cake, Chipped Chocolate Cake, Chocolate Cream Cake, Brown-Eyed Susan Cake, Double-Ring Anniversary Angel Food Cake, Pink Azalea Cake, and Day-at-the-Zoo Cake were born anew as Betty Crocker's product lines evolved to fit the times.

In 1968, General Mills purchased Kenner and its Easy-Bake Oven line. For mother-daughter baking fun, the 1950s Betty Crocker Junior Baking Kit—with tiny animal-shaped cookie cutters—was reintroduced, along with a line of miniature, boxed versions of Betty Crocker mixes for "use in Mom's Oven and in Kenner's Easy-Bake® Oven." In 1973, the oven was officially renamed the "Betty Crocker Easy-Bake Oven" and made available for the first time in Betty's red. Two years later came Stir 'n Frost, a direct descendant of Answer Cake, followed by Super Moist, with pudding in the mix. Betty Crocker even had cakes for the health conscious, with fat-free Sweet Rewards (the 1995 replacement for the 94 percent fat-free Betty Crocker SuperMoist Light

My new Answer Cake

Trade Mark

has its own frosting mix and baking pan right in the package

Here's the box ... look inside ... | Make the cake you'll serve with pride

3 wonderful helpers inside

Luscious cake mix! Superb frosting mix! Ready-to-use cake pan! All in the Answer Cake box. The creamy smooth frosting mix stirs up in just 2 minutes without any cooking at all. The special baking pan doesn't need greasing. It's exactly the right size to make Answer Cake rise to full height and feathery lightness.

4 luscious flavor combinations

White—Yellow—Devils Food Cake—each with Chocolate Fudge Frosting. Peanut Delight Cake with Peanut Crème Frosting.

Makes a 6-serving cake

A new size cake! Just right for smaller families. It makes 6 big, glorious, featherlight pieces. This way you enjoy fresh-tasting cake the _whole_ time you have it. Every crumb is moist — tender — delicious. With Answer Cake you can enjoy fresh cake more often and a variety of flavors, too. A special delight for small families. I do hope you'll try Answer Cake soon!

Answer Cake

answers your cake problems in a new and wonderful way

Betty Crocker had the answers for cooks in need of something more convenient than the "traditional" cake mix.

cake mix). According to Nielsen data, by the late 1990s, 60 percent of households regularly used cake mixes, a significant portion of them bearing the red spoon logo.

Valued at well over a billion dollars—nearly half of that from the dessert-mix unit—the Betty Crocker group consistently ranks among the top twenty brands in food industry surveys. But when it comes to the nostalgia market, Betty's value is probably incalculable. On the occasion of the fiftieth anniversary of Betty Crocker cake mixes in 1998, Christine Arpe Gang recalled in the Memphis *Commercial Appeal,* "I was only a year old when General Mills introduced its first Betty Crocker cake mixes. Like many women of her generation, my mother embraced this convenience product so wholeheartedly she rarely, if ever, made a cake from scratch again."

Chapter Six

Kitchens of the World

His Mother's Oatmeal Cookies

Crispy, nutty-flavored cookies . . . sandwiched together with jelly and jam. Nora M. Young of Cleveland, Ohio, won a prize in the "plain cooky class" on these. Wonderful for lunch box and cooky jar.

Mix together

> **2 cups *sifted* GOLD MEDAL Flour**
>
> **½ tsp. salt**
>
> **3 cups rolled oats**

Cut in until mixture is well blended

> **1 cup shortening (part butter)**

Stir in

> **1 tsp. soda dissolved in ⅓ cup milk (sweet or sour)**
>
> **1½ cups brown sugar**

Chill dough. Roll out ⅛" thick. Cut into desired shapes. Place on ungreased baking sheet. Bake until lightly browned. When cool, and just before serving, put together in pairs with jelly or jam between.

Temperature: 375°   Time: Bake 10 to 12 min.

Amount: About 4 doz. 2½" double cookies.

From *Betty Crocker's Picture Cooky Book, 1948*

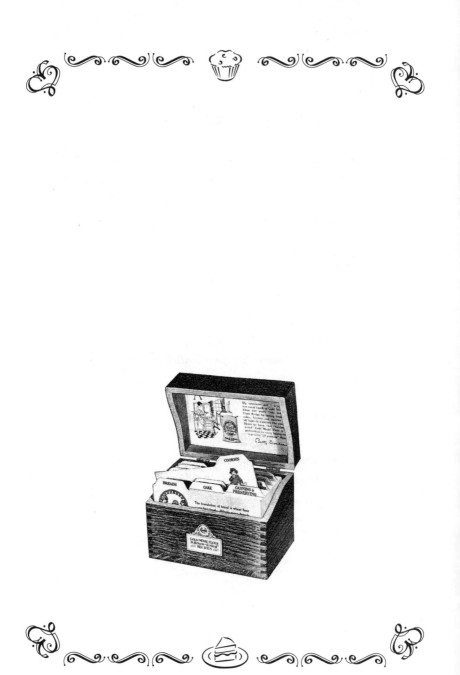

The Betty Crocker Kitchens were once a popular American tourist destination. At least 2 million tourists—U.S. and international—stopped in to pay Betty a visit. Betty's home economists were on hand to demonstrate Betty Crocker's exhaustive recipe-testing procedures, and to deliver baked treats fresh from her oven. Homemakers, clubs, families, church groups, and school-children were just some of the guests. Celebrities like Liberace, the Nixons and Eisenhowers, beauty pageant contestants, and visiting royalty paid their respects to Betty Crocker.

But for some, the Betty Crocker Kitchens experience was a tearful one. "Betty Crocker isn't one woman," visitors were told, "but many women who work here under her name." Receptionists had tissues and sympathy for guests grappling with the cold reality that it was impossible to meet Betty Crocker. Ruby Peterson, a retired General Mills home economist, compares the phenomenon to finding out there is no Santa Claus. People don't usually travel all the way to the North Pole, meet the elves, and then find out the truth about Santa. But what happened at the Betty Crocker Kitchen was "worse because Betty was their hero."

Humble Beginnings

The famous Betty Crocker Kitchens began quite obscurely, in the tiny space between Washburn Crosby's Baker Service Department and its baking laboratory, housed in the chamber of commerce building in downtown Minneapolis. Filling a "long-felt want in the organization" to aid the Home Service Depart-

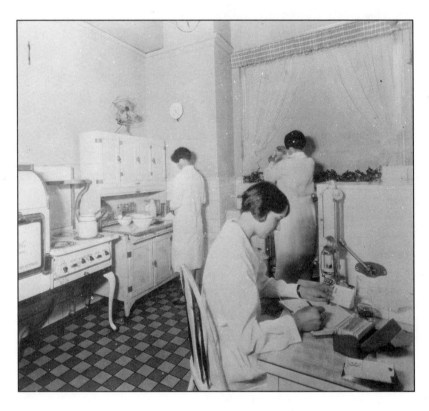

Washburn Crosby's home economists in Betty's first test kitchen in 1924.

ment in recipe development and testing, in 1924 the company added the kind of kitchen that homemakers of the era only dreamed about. According to an internal newsletter, *The Eventually News,* the model kitchen boasted gas and electric ranges, "mechanical refrigeration," and running water. The kitchen's white and Delft-blue color scheme included such functional touches as a writing desk and telephone, the better to conduct Betty Crocker's business on the radio, in print, and through customer relations. It's likely that visitors toured the kitchen, but no count was kept in those early days.

By the mid-1930s test kitchens like Betty's were big business, because sales—of Jell-O gelatin, Kellogg's Corn Flakes, Junket's custard, Hershey's chocolate, PET Milk, and other products—increased dramatically when tested recipes were made available to consumers. A 1934 General Electric food preparation and recipe booklet explained, "In the kitchens of G-E Kitchen Institute, a staff of home economics experts constantly plan and test new and better ways of doing things—under actual home conditions." Modern appliances like GE refrigerators, ranges, broilers, electric mixers, and electric dishwashers were dubbed "the new art of living electrically."

The Campbell's Soup Home Economics Kitchen strove to extend the brand image from reliable—"21 Kinds, 12 Cents a Can"—to adventuresome, with recipes for Gloucester Codfish Balls, Tomato Soup Cake, and Stuffed Eggs with Tomato Rarebit Sauce. Campbell's home economists and chefs created and tested all recipes: "our main concern is the planning of more appetizing and more nourishing meals, and the creating of new and tempting dishes."

McCall's magazine and the H. J. Heinz Company opened their doors to visitors for tours and cooking classes. In a 1930s

Heinz recipe booklet, the company extended an invitation to guests to see for themselves that "quality is paramount" for the best-selling ketchup in the world: "House of HEINZ is proud of its great kitchens as you are of yours. Every year it is our pleasure to escort more than 70,000 visitors through our plant at Pittsburgh so that these visitors may see these kitchens and HEINZ methods in operation."

Kitchen Testing, 1, 2, 3

Within ten years of operation, the Betty Crocker test kitchen evolved into the General Mills Service Kitchens when the staff relocated to the ninth floor of the same building. From 1934 to 1946, Betty's staff continued to grow, expanding its product-testing duties even as the home economists kept on with cooking and baking tests, producing material for the Betty Crocker radio programs, creating recipes for flour inserts and booklets, answering consumer mail, and orchestrating special Depression-era and World War II initiatives. Informal tours of Betty Crocker's kitchens were first initiated at this new location. Betty invited radio listeners to see her new digs and observe her sixteen staff members preparing dishes and serving up meals in the formal dining room, "just as Mrs. Homemaker and her family would have them."

In an October 3, 1934, broadcast, "Celebrating Our Tenth Anniversary in a New Home," Betty Crocker described her new kitchen:

> *We have just moved into a beautiful new home . . . high above the noise and dust of the streets, where we get cross ventilation. The windows on one side of our office look out*

   184

*on the downtown section of Minneapolis. The windows on
the other side, in the kitchen and dining room, give us a
glimpse of the Mississippi River with its bridges, and in the
foreground the big Gold Medal Mills with their huge sign,
"Eventually, Why Not Now?"*

*I'm sure all of you housekeepers can imagine our plea-
sure and delight in having a brand new kitchen, with
everything spic and span and just exactly as we want it.
. . . And we have a welcome mat in our main doorway, put
there for all of you, so if you ever get a chance to come see
us, please do! We are so proud of it all, we love to show it to
those of you who are interested.*

*When we conduct visitors through, we show them the
tasting room first, furnished in Early American furniture,
then on to the kitchen. They all speak of how sunshiny
it looks! The end of the room is entirely taken up with
the sink and tiled drain boards, in various shades of yellow . . . around the border is a simple design in deep blue
tiles. The minute you see it I'm sure those of you who are
loyal users of* SOFTASILK *Cake Flour,* BISQUICK *and*
WHEATIES *will recognize that we have used the same colors in our kitchen that you see in our packaged foods.*

Betty Crocker characterized the décor as charming and
homey; she cited colorful pieces of pottery, Dutch gingham curtains, a paneled archway, a tomato-red watering pot, and a copper
teakettle. But the quaint ambience was almost an afterthought;
the main event was the kitchen's modern amenities:

*Next comes the huge electric refrigerator. We ordered it
unfinished so it could be finished the same color as the rest*

An intimate glimpse into a corner of our gay, peasant kitchen. The color scheme is golden yellow and royal blue. Bright pottery and copper give a homey atmosphere. The little copper cooky molds on either side of the range niche are from Stockholm.

Betty Crocker

An ad for Betty Crocker's *All-Purpose Baking* recipe book included an invitation to tour Betty's kitchens.

of the woodwork. It really looks beautiful. I notice that every man who comes in the kitchen makes immediately for the refrigerator and opens the door and then is properly delighted when the light goes on!

In Betty Crocker's next broadcast, "The Tasting Test," the tour of the Home Service Department's "lovely new quarters" continued, with Betty placing careful emphasis on the dining room's symbiotic relationship with the kitchen. "Wherever there is a kitchen-test of a new recipe, you can imagine there must be a tasting-test too. The old saying still holds true that the 'proof of the pudding is in the eating.' So we have this new and charming little dining room in which to conduct our tasting tests."

"We really do bake all day long," Betty proudly assured her audience. That is "how much testing we actually do."

Not to be outdone, Mary Hale Martin for Libby's explained how her test kitchen yielded "My Best Recipes":

The recipes in this book are not merely KITCHEN-tested— they are DINING ROOM–tested too. I have made up the dishes in my kitchen—very carefully, I assure you—and then, next door in my Early American dining room, they have been served as meals. . . . From the comments of my guests I learn which dishes are generally popular, which seem most unusual and appealing.

Martin claimed herself "unusually fortunate" to conduct such rigorous recipe testing in a charming, homelike atmosphere with knotted pine paneling, leaded casement windows, nice pieces of pewter, copper, and china, and gay hooked rugs.

Betty's staff agreed with its Libby's counterparts that special

Home economists mix it up in Betty's second home on the ninth floor of the chamber of commerce building in downtown Minneapolis.

   188

ONE OF THE FIVE BETTY CROCKER KITCHENS
AT GENERAL MILLS, MINNEAPOLIS, MINN.

Betty Crocker

The Betty Crocker Kitchens are something to write home about.

   189

Triple-testing enabled Betty's staff to guarantee the results of Betty Crocker recipes.

guests—women's magazine editors, representatives from home economics organizations, and food industry colleagues—were best entertained in the dining room. But at Betty's table, innovations in market research were on the menu. The Home Service Department invited unsuspecting General Mills executives to "luncheons" that were experimental taste tests. Home economists never divulged the true intent of the invites, all the better to discerningly observe their guests throughout the meal. "Menfolk" approval of any given recipe cleared it for consumer distribution.

According to the Home Service Department, good recipes didn't just happen. Betty's "famous tested recipes" were the result of the most painstaking kind of culinary work. "Care and thought and science . . . back our products," Betty explained. Recipe ideas typically originated within the department, but some came by way of consumer suggestions. Old standards with plenty of room for variation and improvement were candidates for adaptation. Home economists tested any given recipe about a dozen times, varying the amounts of ingredients and altering baking time and temperature. Once Betty's staff was satisfied with a reworked recipe, home testers continued the process.

As early as 1925, Washburn Crosby employed home testers for recipe trials, commonly known as "Insurance Testing." Homemakers from varying geographic regions and socioeconomic groups were eligible to participate, provided that they held no professional home economics credentials. The rationale was simple: any homemaker, under any set of circumstances, must have the same chance as a professional of succeeding with a recipe. Upon completing each recipe, home testers completed a questionnaire: Did you like the recipe? Did you find it easy or difficult to follow? Was it easy to make or complicated? Were the ingredients too expensive or just right? How would you improve it? How did your family react to the new recipe? Would they want it often—or never again? What were their comments?

Back at the Kitchens, Betty's staff reviewed and compiled the home testers' comments. In this third phase, the home economists used the suggestions of the home testers to finalize the recipe, then performed another series of tests similar to the first round. The goal was to close the margin of error. If the consensus was positive, the recipe became a Betty Crocker Triple-Tested recipe. If not, the recipe was filed away and used for internal recipe research and reference. Triple-Testing epitomized home economic principles applied by the Betty Crocker staff because it practically guaranteed customers cost-effective success. Through Triple-Testing, Betty's staff believed that they were perfecting the equivalent of a "time-tested" and cherished family recipe handed down through generations.

The Polka Dot Kitchen

By 1946, there were once again too many cooks in the Kitchens. That year, Betty's forty-eight staff members set up housekeeping in the General Mills Building in another part of downtown Minneapolis. This new—but certainly not last—incarnation formally took the name Betty Crocker Kitchens. Occupying the entire fifth floor of the building were several themed test kitchens, a large dining room, a terrace, and a spacious reception area for cooking demonstrations and screenings of food-related films—as well as a large editorial office, a mail division, a radio division, and a library.

For staff members, workdays began in the dressing room. Individual hatboxes, coat hangers, and cubbyholes stored personal

items, and full-length mirrors were available for last-minute checks before one emerged into the public spaces as a "Crockette," as staffers fondly called one another. Tour groups large and small—made up mostly of women—visited the Kitchens year-round, eager for a taste of Betty's world-class hospitality. Guests entered an inviting blue-and-yellow reception area, where they were greeted, relieved of their coats and hats, and offered refreshments. While they waited for the tours to assemble, they were welcome to browse Betty's extensive library of cookbooks or ask the home economists questions about baking.

One showcase was the large, light blue Terrace Kitchen, used for general testing and meal preparation for specialty luncheons. "Terrace," so called for its adjoining faux patio terrace, complete with "garden furniture," was equipped with a window where visitors could observe the "hum of activity." The baking unit was outfitted with every conceivable ingredient and utensil; specially designed cabinets had a roll-up door for spices, slots for cookie sheets, and built-in flour sifters. Tourists were notorious for opening drawers and peeking into cupboards, hoping for a glimpse of Betty's secrets.

Also on display was the ever busy Kitchen of Tomorrow, two kitchens in one. Decorated with Swedish motifs, Tomorrow was equipped with a combination of older and state-of-the-art appliances. One side of the kitchen was reserved for experimental baking and the development of new methods and new products—such as Betty Crocker's Crust*quick*—while the other was the domain of General Mills' quality-minded Products Control division. The most unusual feature of this double kitchen was a huge rotating stainless-steel oven able to accommodate ten to twelve cakes simultaneously. The oven's motion generated air circulation ideal for cake baking and thus for testing recipes.

  193

The "gayest" of Betty's kitchens—Polka Dot—was used to test her line of small appliances.

   194

The Kamera Kitchen had three self-contained work units where food stylists prepped food for advertisements, promotions, recipe booklets, and package labels. As the photographers snapped away, Betty's staff worked diligently to save their works of art from melting away under the hot lights. In Kamera, the emphasis was not on taste but on appearance. However, General Mills' tradition of high standards barred nonfood material—like shaving cream standing in for whipped cream—in photo shoots, so stylists had to work quickly and efficiently with the photographers to ensure appetizing images. If the photographs didn't turn out just right, Betty's staff went back to the beginning and started from scratch.

Betty's most crowd-pleasing kitchen was her red and white Polka Dot Kitchen, described as the "gayest, most colorful of all." The polka-dot theme extended to appliance literature, packaging, and advertising, and the inherent playfulness of the color scheme made it a perennial tour favorite. The testing site for Betty Crocker's line of home appliances, such as the Betty Crocker Thru-Heat Iron and Pressure-Quick Saucepan, Polka Dot had a glossy sheen, heightened by the "stainless steel counters and a laundry unit for experimental work with appliances."

Guests clamored for samples from the popular Tasting Bar, where home economists set out their day's work. From there it was on to the formal dining room, three times bigger than in Betty's previous kitchen, but consistent with its early American design. With its paneling salvaged from a New England house of the 1750s, rustic open-hearth fireplace, antique chairs, dough box, and old pewter utensils, the room was a "surprising contrast to the up-to-the-minute kitchens."

Tours of Betty's Kitchens were free of charge, but high demand meant appointments were required. Between the years of

1948 and 1953, at least 26,519 visitors signed the guest book, which is likely not a full accounting. But the volumes of visitors did not alter the Kitchens' focus—testing recipes. By 1949, it was estimated that more than a *billion* copies of Betty Crocker's tested recipes were distributed yearly. The continuous high demand for recipes and new General Mills products kept Betty's staff increasing and the Kitchens active beyond capacity.

Home of Betty Crocker

In 1958, the Betty Crocker Kitchens relocated to the sprawling grounds of General Mills' new headquarters in the Minneapolis suburb of Golden Valley. Betty welcomed a new round of guests: "Come into our kitchen and see how we test and develop recipes, work on new products and perfect quicker, easier methods to help you in your homemaking." The new Kitchens— Homemaker Kitchen (a Terrace Kitchen look-alike), Kamera Kitchen, Quality Kitchen, and Experimental Kitchens—were similar in structure and design to their culinary predecessors. The formal dining room once again entertained visitors while recipe testing and food preparation continued in the surrounding kitchens.

Of the sixty workers at the Betty Crocker Kitchens, more than half were home economists. The rest performed administrative duties, conducted tours, and kept up with consumer correspondence. As the 1950s drew to a close, Betty wasn't as popular around the post office as she had been in previous years. Where at her peak she had received 4,000 to 5,000 letters a day, she now got about 10,000 a month. That total remained impressive by any standard, but especially considering that Betty's radio and television programming had ended years before.

The American Home Economics Association made a pilgrimage to Betty's Kitchens circa 1965.

Betty in Red

"Food is perhaps America's biggest weapon in the Cold War," pronounced *Life* magazine in January 1955. In 1959, Betty and her Kitchens ventured behind the Iron Curtain to put that theory to the test. As leaders in America's $73 billion food industry, General Mills and General Foods were invited by the U.S. government to participate in a U.S. Trade and Cultural Fair in Moscow. More than seven tons of food, including cake mixes, frozen fruits, juices, and vegetables were shipped for use during the six-week demonstration of sped-up meal preparation, American style—"quick 'n' easy," "heat and serve."

From eleven in the morning until nine at night, both companies staged continuous presentations in their joint exhibition space in Sokolniki Park. The Model Kitchen fascinated and entertained a steady stream of Russian visitors, many of whom watched a cake-baking demonstration from start to finish, which could be as long as two hours, including cool-down time. Interpreters kept busy answering questions directed at home economists about pastel-tinted macaroons, colored icing, birthday candles, and paper baking cups for muffins. The Russian government did not allow any sampling of the food, but occasionally a brownie or two would disappear when no one was looking.

Some fairgoers were so impressed with the demonstrations that they showered the home economists with flowers. Premier Nikita Khrushchev, on the other hand, disapproved wholeheartedly. The Model Kitchen was the setting for the infamous "Kitchen Debate" between him and Vice President Richard Nixon. The politicians exchanged angry words over the gleaming kitchen appliances, which Nixon touted as a "showcase for democracy," explaining, "We have many different manufacturers and many different kinds of washing machines so that the housewives have a choice." Khrushchev countered, with the full chill of the Cold War, "Many of the things you have shown us are interesting but are not needed in life."

Follow the Red Spoons

Back on American soil, Betty's kitchens once again outgrew their space. In August 1966, General Mills launched their grand re-opening in a new wing of the headquarters. Open to the public—who were directed to "Follow the Red Spoons" toward the newly renamed Betty Crocker Kitchens of the World—the elaborate, two-week celebration included a commemorative filmstrip, re-freshments, and guided tours of seven separate kitchens repre-senting seven regions famous for their cuisine. The California Kitchen, in shades of vermilion, pale lavender, and sky blue, cele-brated western outdoor living with its hooded barbecue grill, garden tools, and hanging plants festooned over a white brick-patterned floor and latticework. The window in the Mediter-ranean Kitchen "looked out" on a mural of Italy's famous Amalfi Drive. Mediterranean had a faux wine cellar, and sea-green ceramic tile complemented the bright blue floors.

Housing the Betty Crocker antique collection, the New En-gland Kitchen continued the tradition of kitchens past with chestnut cabinetry, a beamed ceiling, oak plank floor, and a fire-place oven. The Latin American "Kitchen of the Sun" was awash in yellow, vibrant pink, oranges, and foliage greens. A sunny motif and Spanish mission arches completed the theme. By con-trast, the simple Scandinavian Kitchen drew its effect from nat-ural wood beams and lobster-colored countertops. The cabinets

  199

were painted in a shrimp-bisque hue identical to the hand-stenciled border designs representing Scandinavian crafts, decorative eggs, bread, straw brooms, and pottery.

The New Orleans Kitchen evoked the French Quarter with ornate black patio lanterns and a black grillwork gate opening to a painted garden scene. Cabinets were in hyacinth blue, the wallcovering chintz. The Oriental Kitchen's colors were inspired by the cobalt blue and white of Asian porcelains. The vinyl floor resembled a stone path and the orange Japanese apothecary chest allegedly dated back to the 1840s. Bamboo ceiling, teakwood furnishings, and a "view" of a cherry tree in full bloom added a "touch of Oriental beauty." While a Camera-Ready Kitchen had been installed in another part of the building, an eighth Kitchen, unthemed, was used for food demonstrations for General Mills' marketing executives and advertising agencies. All eight kitchens had the same floor plan; they boasted gas and electric ranges and several microwave ovens. Refrigerators and freezers were concealed behind decorative panels.

In 1977, the Betty Crocker Kitchens of the World gave way to the Betty Crocker American Family Kitchens, including new American themes: Chinatown Kitchen, Williamsburg Kitchen, Pennsylvania Dutch Kitchen, Hawaiian Kitchen, Arizona Desert Kitchen, and Cape Cod Kitchen. Over the next several years the Kitchens occasionally changed names and underwent renovations, keeping pace with America's changing eating habits. But on January 15, 1985, the unthinkable happened. The Betty Crocker Kitchens closed their doors to the public, seemingly forever. The decision reflected the increasing difficulty of preserving the confidentiality of General Mills' product research while providing high-quality tours. In the period just before the closing, as many as five kitchens would have to be closed off during

One of Betty Crocker's several American-themed kitchens in 1977.

   201

any given tour to protect product development secrets, leaving visitors with a not-so-behind-the-scenes perspective.

The press took the Kitchens closing hard. One local journalist wrote of a chill wind blowing from General Mills with the news of the closing. "We don't harbor such cozy images of any other food company's kitchens, probably because only in Betty Crocker did we find a corporate symbol who was also a friend. I don't identify with the Pillsbury Doughboy, nor would I think of writing him for a recipe. But Betty Crocker is mother, teacher, big sister and grandmother rolled into one—a member of the family—and somehow I always expected her door to be open." As about eighteen "Crockettes" hung up their docent smocks, the Kitchens turned entirely toward recipe and product testing.

Yet echoes of the Kitchens lingered. Sylvia Paine, who had never been inside, was in mourning for the loss. "Reports from the few people I know who visited the seven kitchens leave me yearning. They speak of the Hawaiian room, the Southwestern room, of multiple microwave ovens and of clever magnetic strips to hold recipes at eye level. They recall glamorous women measuring everything with precision, cooking colorful, imaginative meals from scratch."

Even though Betty's home remained off limits to the public, honored guests were occasionally invited to the inner sanctum. One such guest, Ms. Eddie Murphy of Buena Park, California, experienced a baking dream of a lifetime in 1996. As one of seventy-five finalists in the "Spirit of Betty Crocker" contest, Murphy was invited on an insiders' tour of Betty's Kitchens. "Everything is color coordinated," Murphy said, recalling the kitchens. "It smelled heavenly—chocolate, baked goods."

Kitchens Redux

In the fall of 2003, the Betty Crocker Kitchens welcomed visitors once again. The 2001 merger of General Mills and Pillsbury had necessitated a completely new kitchen facility to reflect the melding of the Betty Crocker Kitchens and Pillsbury Test Kitchens staff. And after two years of development, planning, and construction, and the spending of millions of dollars, General Mills couldn't help but show off Betty's new home, America's most technologically and conceptually advanced kitchen showcase. Several times a year, the Kitchens host an open house, complete with tours and a cooking lesson from Betty's expert staff.

Betty's newest Kitchens occupy a grand total of 13,595 square feet at General Mills' headquarters. In a wing of their very own, twenty home economists and eight technicians test 50,000 recipes a year. Built to withstand eight hours of baking and cooking daily, Betty Crocker Kitchens are truly extraordinary, with 19 fully equipped kitchens, 18 tons of polished Kashmir White granite countertops, over 1,500 linear feet of custom-built cabinets in a West African makore-wood veneer, 18 refrigerators, 15 freezers, 50 ovens, 6 speed-cook ovens, 22 microwaves, 31 cooktops (250 total burners!), and 19 dishwashers (14 conventional and 5 flash models).

Five of the largest kitchens occupy a two-story atrium and look out on the company's vast courtyard. These kitchens are devoted to recipe development for Pillsbury and Betty Crocker cookbooks and supermarket magazines. A dozen adjacent kitchens are used for product testing and development, with one dedicated to Pillsbury Bake-Off recipes. One kitchen designed for media broadcasts features nonreflective countertops and cab-

Betty Crocker's newly remodeled kitchens in 2003.

inetry. Betty's dining room comes equipped with a demonstration kitchen and a gallery of her portraits through the years. The Kitchens also include America's largest corporate cookbook library. Home economists conduct recipe and food trend research using the 9,000 titles, which occupy 1,260 feet of high-density, easy-access rolling bookshelves.

Geographic themes, polka dots, tie-back curtains, fake scenery, and antiques have given way to a muted but sophisticated decorating style. The colorful exception is a dignified glass mosaic wall, where a blue panel to represent Pillsbury matches a red representing Betty Crocker. Otherwise, form follows function, with wireless PC portals and discreet pop-up ventilation systems. With wide aisles and open design that foster collaboration, clutterless workspaces, and shock-absorbent flooring in Marmoleum, the entire facility is ergonomically designed to accommodate every need of the Betty Crocker Kitchens staff. But even as the immaculate appliances glimmer and glint, they can't stop the passage of time. Unlike Betty herself, her home will be only about ten years old when it begins to show the sorrowful signs of age.

Chapter Seven

*Strangely
Familiar*

Chocolate Joy Cake

(. . . like creamy fudge . . . so smooth and velvety . . .)

3 sq. chocolate (3 oz.)	3 tsp. baking powder
½ cup hot water	¼ tsp. soda
½ cup shortening	½ tsp. salt
1⅔ cups sugar	1 cup sour milk or
3 eggs	buttermilk

2 cups GOLD MEDAL "Kitchen-tested" Flour

METHOD—Mix shaved chocolate with hot water and cook to thick paste, stirring constantly . . . about 3 to 5 minutes. Set aside to cool. Cream shortening, add sugar gradually and cream thoroughly. Beat eggs well and blend into the creamed mixture. Add the *cooled* chocolate mixture and blend well. Sift flour once before measuring. Sift flour, baking powder, soda and salt together and add to the creamed mixture alternately with the sour milk. Pour into well greased and floured layer pans. Bake. When cake is cool, spread Chocolate Icing between the layers and over top and sides of cake. *Time*—Bake 30 to 35 minutes. *Temperature*—350° F, moderate oven. *Size of Pans*—Two 9-inch round layer pans.

CHOCOLATE ICING

6 tbsp. shortening

1 egg yolk

3 cups confectioners' sugar

4 tbsp. cocoa

3 to 4 tbsp. hot water

METHOD—Cream shortening and blend in the egg yolk. Sift sugar and cocoa together and add alternately with the hot water. Beat until smooth.

From *New Editions of Old Favorites Men Like,* by Betty Crocker, 1938

Betty Crocker made a name for herself long before she got a face. In Betty's days as a radio star, hearing was believing— believing that Betty was a person genuinely helpful with cooking and other domestic matters. Her modern sensibilities were the perfect complement to her old-fashioned manners. She was even a bit glamorous, keeping company as she did with Hollywood movie stars. At the same time, Betty was a bit of mystery, because no one could be sure what she looked like.

Bettys We Hardly Knew

Three faces of Betty emerged during her first decade, in the service of radio and product promotions. With slight variations, her youthful visage—its oval shape recalling a Victorian cameo silhouette; her short marcelled hair a nod to the modern professionalism of the home economics movement—smiled from magazine ads and recipe booklets for Gold Medal Flour, Softas-Silk Cake Flour, and Bisquick. A 1930 painting on brick showed Betty speaking into her mike: "Baking secrets by radio."

Yet even as the Betty Crocker persona boosted sales of General Mills products, an enigma factor remained. Consumers, many of whom knew Betty best from her voice over the radio, hoped for a greater intimacy with the homemakers' heroine. More and more of the thousands of daily letters to Betty Crocker included requests for her photograph. The Home Service staff found themselves "creatively" sidestepping the issue with the

211

explanation that Betty Crocker didn't like having her photograph taken. By the mid-1930s, the stage was set to finally put an official face with the household name.

Ageless Thirty-two

To commemorate the momentous occasion of Betty's fifteenth anniversary in 1936, General Mills commissioned a portrait from the New York commercial artist Neysa McMein, best known for her work with *McCall's*. From 1923 through 1937, McMein contributed monthly covers for the magazine and wrote opinion pieces as well. In 1926, "two of the nation's most prominent mothers"—McMein and the famous dancer Irene Castle (who set the bobbed-hair trend in America)—staged a debate in *McCall's* pages. The question: "Ought mothers give up careers for babies?" Neysa McMein, whose married name was Baragwanath, answered a definitive no. "I am too much addicted both to motherhood and to paid work to stand by and see either of them cheated," McMein, one of the nation's "most prominent mothers," passionately decreed. "I will wait right here while you name me six reasons a woman can't divide her life fairly between them."

While Betty Crocker, in her own fashion, would go on to echo McMein's support for women's work outside the home, there the association ended. McMein was an urban sophisticate who didn't know how to cook, hosted a nightly salon in her studio across from Carnegie Hall, and kept a whiskey still in her bathroom. Yet, with her midwestern roots, she was attracted to the challenge of interpreting the homemaking expert from America's heartland, already idealized by millions for qualities they had never actually seen.

   212

One of several early, unofficial Betty Crocker portraits.

However, capturing the essence of Betty proved a formidable endeavor, even for the likes of McMein. Her first attempt was met with a lukewarm reception from General Mills executives. According to Betty lore, McMein's revisions took an unusual tack: she made a composite of several physical features of the Gold Medal Home Service staff. This portrait was enthusiastically approved, then unveiled with great ceremony in November of 1936. McMein's Betty debuted on a national scale in a magazine ad offering an anniversary gift—free copies of "Betty Crocker's 15 Prize Recipes." Approximately 5 million customers took the company up on its offer, receiving not only the booklet

An unofficial Betty Crocker portrait (1925),
used in her radio show advertisements.

but a coupon "good for one colored reproduction of Betty Crocker's new painting by Neysa McMein, famous magazine cover artist."

In McMein's rendition, Betty Crocker's head and shoulders emerge from a cloudy canvas background in a style that recalls colonial portraiture. Her face is regal, with tight bow lips and haunting slate-blue eyes; her short dark hair is streaked with gray. According to the General Mills historian James Gray, McMein gave Betty "a fine Nordic brow and shape of skull, a jaw of slightly Slavic resolution and features that might be claimed contentedly by various European groups—eyes, Irish; nose,

Pre-McMein version of Betty Crocker.

   215

The first official portrait of Betty Crocker, created by Neysa McMein in 1936.

General Mills vice president Sam Gale was known as the "father of Betty Crocker."

classic Roman—the perfect composite of the twentieth-century American woman."

While McMein's Betty, with her serious, remote expression, may reflect the cares of her era, Betty's admirers were simply and instantly smitten. "You look exactly like I thought you would!" one woman excitedly wrote to Betty upon first glimpse. Letter after letter poured out enthusiasm for the long-awaited sight of Betty's face on food packaging and in print advertisements. Exuding authority, confidence, and an eagerness to help her customers, Betty seemed every inch a real woman.

In the press, Betty was pegged as "an ageless 32." While McMein's technique (she was known for her work with pastels) may have softened her features, most would agree that thirty-two is a bit of a stretch. No matter. Endowed with a voice, a personality—some would say a heart—and now a recognizable face, Betty Crocker took a step closer to lifelike status.

To date, McMein's Betty Crocker is the longest-running portrait, having survived almost twenty years. The wardrobe palette McMein devised—vivid red with white accents—has never been altered in any subsequent official portrait. Yet many unofficial visions of Betty remain tucked away in the recesses of the General Mills archives. Several interpretations of the McMein paintings reveal at least half a body, as Betty sits to serve food at a table or stands at her recipe files. She smiles broadly in one version and wears a *green*-and-white outfit in another. During the 1940s and the early 1950s, several of these variations found their way into recipe booklets, packaging, and print advertising campaigns. McMein's distinctive style offers artistic insurance. Her subject, perfectly poised for a cup of coffee and a chat, is unmistakably Betty Crocker.

As Seen on TV

By 1948—just three years after Betty Crocker was named the second most popular woman in America—a million American homes had television sets. Betty was already a multimedia star in Hollywood and on radio; it was only a matter of time before she conquered television. And with television sales expanding by 600 percent that year—to a total of 2 million sets nationwide by August—the moment was fast approaching.

But who would play Betty? General Mills' James S. Fish, who in 1955 would be elevated to advertising director, was highly involved in the selection process. "I want to be remembered as the guy who fought for Betty Crocker," Fish was quoted as saying. The logical leading candidates were the many actresses who over the years had given Betty her radio voice—Zella Layne, Betty Bucholz, and Adelaide Hawley. Each was invited to screen-test for the part.

None of the actresses resembled McMein's Betty—Hawley, for example, was "stunningly blonde." Yet Hawley offered a particularly intriguing intangible, "a dream in her eyes all women will be quick to recognize." Audiences spotted it immediately, awarding Hawley's screen tests top marks, and landing her, along with understudies Madelon Mitchell and Jane Webb, the role of a lifetime. "I am the current incarnation of a corporate image," Hawley told the press.

From 1950 to 1958, Hawley as Betty starred in several cooking shows and variety programs. Her half-hour *Betty Crocker Show* aired on CBS from 1950 to 1952, followed by the *Betty Crocker Star Matinee* and *Bride and Groom,* both for ABC, in 1952. There was also *Time for Betty Crocker,* a fifteen-minute dramatization of letters to Betty. In 1952, Hawley made televi-

  219

Several actresses and home economists played the role of Betty Crocker on radio and television, but Adelaide Hawley stole the spotlight with her memorable television appearances on *The George Burns and Gracie Allen Show.*

sion history by appearing as Betty Crocker in CBS's very first color commercial (CBS's color technology had been approved as the national standard in October 1950). Betty Crocker even made the cast list of *The George Burns and Gracie Allen Show*. From 1955 to 1958—seasons five through eight of the series— Betty took her cue from such lines as "I don't know how to bake a cake, Gracie, but here is Betty Crocker to show us how." Live, during the sponsor breaks, Hawley "taught" Burns and Allen to use a simple and easy Betty Crocker cake mix. Hawley—playing it straight—seamlessly contributed to the famous couple's comedy routine, consoling Allen on her poor cooking skills, assuring her that even she could succeed with Betty Crocker products.

Betty's years on the small screen coincided with the exponential growth of television; in 1950, 8 million American homes had sets; in 1958, the figure was 41 million. But Betty's television shows never came close to equaling her radio programs, either commercially or financially. By the late 1950s, they had all been canceled in favor of commercial spots. Hawley's association with General Mills ended in 1964; she went on to earn a doctoral degree in speech education from New York University in 1967. Upon Hawley's passing in 1998, General Mills eulogized, "Certainly she was a broadcasting pioneer and probably the most visible Betty of all time."

The Business End of Betty's Spoon

Betty—who, between Marjorie Child Husted and Adelaide Hawley, was not unfamiliar with stand-ins—was spelled in 1954 by a different sort of pinch hitter, a red spoon logo embellished with her signature. The design firm Lippincott & Margulies was

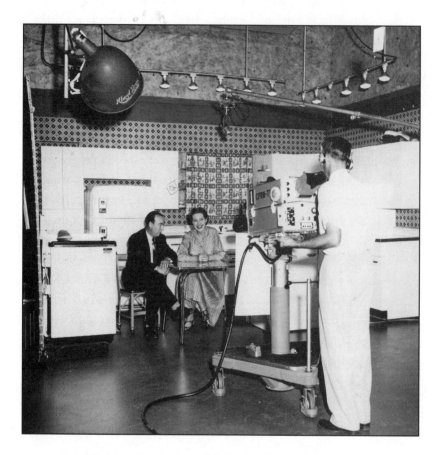

Actress Adelaide Hawley as Betty Crocker films a television spot.

hired by General Mills to create this visual shorthand for Betty's image, trademark, and customer services. Given a prominent place on Betty Crocker food packaging, the red spoon befits Betty's longtime association with the kitchen, and the mixing done there every day. With its smooth and rounded dimensions, the spoon is universally suitable for infants and adults, unlike the sharp-edged knife or pointy-pronged fork. And, unlike the human representation of Betty, a spoon has no wardrobe or hairstyle to go out of date. A 1988 *Forbes* profile strongly hinted at the corporate tensions surrounding Betty's perpetual portrait makeovers. "Of the two"—Betty's face and the logo—"the red spoon is the more attractive," one executive joked anonymously. Today the red spoon graces more than 200 products.

Grandma Betty

Around the time Betty made her television debut, McMein's Betty fell from grace. The discrepancies between Betty as seen on TV and Betty as seen on cake mix boxes were just far too great. Extensive market research conducted in 1953 by the psychologists Ernest Dichter and Burleigh Gardner concluded that a Depression-era Betty did not suit the new prosperous postwar America. An elaborate two-year search for the perfect new Betty Crocker ensued. By 1954, six commissioned artists, including Norman Rockwell, painted their interpretations of America's First Lady of Food. The six portraits, plus McMein's version and a portrait of Adelaide Hawley, were presented to a cross-section of 1,600 homemakers, who were asked to consider: Would you want her as a friend? Does she look honest? Does she look like a housewife or a career woman? Does she look relaxed or tense?

The photograph of Hawley placed a high third, Rockwell's version came in a close second, and the artist Hilda Taylor's rendition of Betty Crocker took the proverbial cake.

Taylor's Betty, unveiled in 1955, is the version that many Baby Boomers fondly remember from childhood. The new Betty appeared older, friendlier, softer-looking, and more grandmotherly. Like McMein's version, Taylor's Betty is wearing red and white; her eyes are blue, her hair streaked with gray. In stark contrast is Taylor's transformation of Betty's complexion to ruddy and glowing. Taylor painted a series of Betty Crocker portraits, at least three of which were used officially by General Mills. In one ver-

Norman Rockwell and five other artists were commissioned to paint new portraits of Betty Crocker for public selection in 1955.

sion, Betty is smiling, but with a closed mouth. In another, Betty is showing some teeth, with a broad, bright smile. The third and final version—Betty in three-quarter profile—captures in Betty's sidelong glance some of the same mystique suggested in McMein's version. Taylor's neighbor and friend Muriel Wadsworth posed for the portrait and has spent a lifetime hearing that there is something strangely familiar about her face.

Dramatic Departures

Taylor's Grandma Betty reigned for ten years, but in the 1960s was undone by America's growing glorification of youth. In 1964, Mercedes Bates became the new director of the Betty Crocker Kitchens; one of her first acts was to plan the dethroning of Queen Betty for a younger Princess Betty. Bates's reasoning was simple: Betty Crocker was out-of-date and her matronly image was inaccessible to younger customers. "Aside from the fact that copies of the portrait hang in some of our sales offices and in the main lobby, we have moved farther and farther away from the presentation of a real live Betty Crocker figure. It's a change in the times . . . because since the radio days, we have never really personified Betty Crocker."

Bates engaged her former staff at *McCall's* to make over Betty Crocker. A model who looked like Taylor's Betty was flown from Minneapolis to New York, where top beauty professionals cut and dyed her hair, then updated its style, along with her makeup, clothes, and jewelry. Countless photographs of the model in her Betty best were handed over to a *McCall's* illustrator, Joe Bowler, who was charged with creating a Betty Crocker fit for a new generation.

   225

Hilda Taylor's portrait (one of three she made) was deemed the best suited to Betty's persona.

Taylor's 1955 Betty Crocker portrait shows some teeth.

   227

Taylor's 1955 profile of Betty Crocker.

In 1965, Bowler introduced a "dramatic departure" from Betty's past. With a few strokes of the paintbrush, Betty lost ten to fifteen years and pounds, gaining sophistication and polish. She wears a red suit with three strands of white pearls around her neck, à la Jacqueline Kennedy. Her dark brown hair has auburn highlights, and her grays are gone. Her perfectly oval face just hints at a smile. Most distinctly, Betty Crocker does not look as if she spends any time at all in the kitchen—at the symphony, perhaps, but not in the kitchen. One writer suggested that it would be more appropriate to call her "Elizabeth rather than Betty." It's hard to say if younger homemakers related to this Betty, especially since her image was rarely used on food packages and advertisements. Instead, General Mills' advertisers favored the simplicity and easy recognition of the red spoon with Betty's signature.

Nevertheless, Betty was updated again four years later. James S. Fish, who by this time had succeeded Sam Gale as the company's advertising director, maintained that updating Betty's portrait was the best way to keep Betty Crocker alive, vibrant, and attuned to the modern generation. Again, Bates consulted her *McCall's* colleagues for advice on hair, makeup, and fashion, inviting Bowler to update Betty Crocker but not reinvent her. After careful consideration, Betty Crocker's creative team instructed Bowler to take the "bubble" out of her hairstyle, ditch the pearls, add an ascot, lighten up the lipstick, emphasize the eyes, and deemphasize the eyebrows.

Bowler's modified Betty, completed in 1969, met with mixed reviews. Bowler's 1969 Betty (often misdated as 1968), has a softer look with more-tanned skin. One journalist referred in retrospect to the 1969 Betty as a "dead ringer for Mary Tyler Moore." Though her expression is vaguely sensuous and the set

Betty Crocker's 1965 "presidential" portrait update, by magazine illustrator Joe Bowler.

Betty Crocker's 1969 (often misdated as 1968) portrait update, by Bowler.

of her eyes uneven, this Betty never deviates from the traditions of her sisters—red-and-white dress, brown hair, and blue eyes. Betty's earrings are by Monet—then a subsidiary of General Mills—and her overall style reflects a fashionable 1960s alternative to hippie chic. As with McMein's Betty, there is a ghostly antiquated quality to the way the edges of her suit disappear into a milky white background. While not a stranger to the kitchen, neither does this version of Betty look intimately acquainted with the place.

By 1972, plans were under way for yet another makeover, the third in seven years. The creative staff behind Betty's last two updates decided that a new portrait was long overdue, given that more women than ever before were graduating from colleges and universities, establishing careers in the paid workforce, and participating in politics. Accordingly, emphasis was to be placed on the American woman's significant role outside the home. Consultation with trend experts yielded a more businesslike look for Betty Crocker. But before General Mills could go public with the new portrait, a made-for-media protest tarnished Betty's otherwise squeaky-clean image.

Betty Crocker at Large

In July 1972, the Minneapolis–St. Paul chapter of the National Organization of Women (NOW) filed a class action complaint against General Mills, charging that Betty Crocker's portrait was both racist and sexist. According to NOW's attorney, "Betty Crocker is an image that women are expected to live up to—a stereotyped image. She is not an image that many women can identify with." Betty Crocker's Caucasian representation was viewed by NOW as discriminatory toward minority women. The outspoken Minneapolis journalist Barbara Flanagan responded in her column, "To me and to most women, Betty Crocker is just another advertising gimmick. I find it no more threatening to my ego than the Campbell Kids." She questioned NOW's priorities and wondered out loud why the organization wasn't targeting Julia Child for being a white woman who cooks. Several more local journalists echoed Flanagan's sentiments, claiming that deconstructing and villainizing Betty was not the answer, suggesting that NOW focus on the denial of equal rights and employment opportunities for women.

The debate is potent and compelling on both sides, making it difficult to view Betty strictly through the either/or lenses of right/wrong, black/white, sinner/saint, good witch/bad witch. Critics of Betty Crocker are not far from wrong in claiming that stereotypes can be toxic, that they distort reality and can perpetuate harmful prejudices. NOW's criticism of Betty Crocker stems from a political strategy within the women's liberation movement of publicly smashing highly visible cultural icons—such as Betty Crocker—that represent a limited view of women.

Yet many women claimed that Betty Crocker was empowering and genuinely helpful in their time of need. And many more took from Betty what they needed—whatever was convenient—discarding the rest and never buying into the idea that Betty Crocker's face represented all a woman could be.

Within a couple of months the media lost interest in the NOW–versus–Betty Crocker controversy and Betty's 1972 portrait update was back on schedule. The Minnesota artist Jerome Ryan captured Betty the businesswoman in a red David Crystal suit (another erstwhile subsidiary of General Mills), over a frilly white blouse, Monet pin, and fussy hair. Her vibrant blue eyes

Betty Crocker's 1972 portrait update, by Jerome Ryan.

aged slightly and her expression is rather subdued. Some say that the 1972 Betty resembles another First Lady—Lady Bird Johnson—though in this particular guise the First Lady of Food spent more time in the kitchen than in the public eye. Betty's portrait hung in the lobby of the Betty Crocker Kitchens, along with four other official Betty portraits. She was featured in some cookbooks, but most of the products bearing Betty Crocker's name were portrait-free.

In 1980, the whole familiar cycle started up again, with Betty's executives despairing anew that her 1972 hair, makeup, and clothes were hopelessly outdated for the thirty-something target market. This time, however, General Mills dispensed with beauty experts and market researchers and turned to Madison Avenue. A Manhattan design team delivered a 1980s beauty with full lips, a short, wavy hairdo, and a simple, understated red-and-white outfit.

Six years later, General Mills chose the New York artist Harriet Pertchik to do the honors. Pertchik had already successfully updated such advertising characters as Mama Celeste and Blue Bonnet Sue, and her preliminary sketches of Betty challenged a few ingrained notions. One concept imagined Betty dressed in a *white* suit and *red* blouse, though that did not meet with company approval. Like so many artists before her, Pertchik was asked to retouch the portrait, this time to add some "character lines" around Betty's eyes and mouth.

In Pertchik's final version, Betty's blue eyes changed to a glimmering green. Dainty gold hoop earrings and golden highlights complete the picture. Around her neck is an impossible white bow that one observer called a "fire hazard over a hot stove." Betty's head is tilted to the side and she's wearing a slightly crooked smile, an expression that inspired one observer

   235

Betty Crocker's 1980 portrait update, by a New York design firm.

Betty Crocker's 1986 portrait update, by Harriet Pertchik.

   237

to remark that Betty looks as though she might have her mind on something other than cupcakes. A General Mills press release calls Pertchik's Betty "a professional woman, approachable, friendly, competent and as comfortable in the boardroom as she is in the dining room." Since she had seemingly been freed from kitchen duty, Betty's white bow was out of harm's way.

The press never seems to grow tired of Betty Crocker's face-lift stories. "Betty Crocker at 65 Looks Like a Million Bucks" headlined the *Minneapolis Star-Tribune* report that the 1986 makeover cost about a million dollars, factoring in "extensive consumer research," and "the cost of developing cookbooks packaging her new image." Several journalists called Betty a "yuppie" while others extolled the virtues of her new lifelike appearance. It did not escape notice that Betty Crocker had turned sixty-five yet never looked younger. She looks "a little bit like . . . the librarian-like Betty of the late 40s and the Betty-bobs-her-hair version of the 50s," explained the National Public Radio newscaster Linda Wertheimer. But there was a "real problem" with the 1986 Betty Crocker: "She [is] younger than me. I hate that! . . . Whatever she looks like, she better be at least Betty of the Baby Boomers or I will have to disassociate myself." While Wertheimer's portrait dates were off, her point, that we have definite ideas of how Betty should look, was right on.

A major factor in the renewed interest in Betty was the reintroduction of her portrait in magazine and newspaper advertisements. In 1988, Betty resumed her former role as spokesperson with a two-page ad in Sunday coupon circulars, which prominently featured Betty's portrait with the headline "The First Lady of Desserts, Re-Elected America's #1 Dessert Choice," along with coupons for Supreme Brownie Mix, Wild Blueberry Muffin Mix, SuperMoist Cake Mix, and Creamy Deluxe Frosting, all with the red spoon logo. An entirely new generation got a peek at the elusive Betty Crocker, with her portrait suggesting that if you can see her, she must be real.

The Spirit of Betty Crocker

To commemorate Betty's platinum anniversary in 1996, General Mills kicked off a year-long celebration of all things Betty Crocker. The Betty Crocker 75th Anniversary Diamond Sweepstakes yielded one sweet story. Twenty-two-year-old Jeff Joerger, a construction worker from Cedar Falls, Iowa, was the first of seventy-five to win the grand prize: a .75-carat diamond pendant necklace. "I buy Betty Crocker brownies all the time and I didn't even know there was a contest going on," Joerger said. He planned to have the diamond, appraised at $4,000, reset as an engagement ring for his fiancée. Joerger pledged his ongoing loyalty to Betty Crocker brownie mixes "because they're easy to make and taste great."

The main event, the Spirit of Betty Crocker essay contest, required more skill than luck. Contest organizers called for seventy-five women—"ages 18 to 118" and living in North America—to be the inspiration for the new Betty Crocker portrait. Each application, whether submitted by an individual herself or on behalf of a loved one, was held to strict criteria. The nominee was required to submit a personal photograph, the name of a favorite Betty Crocker recipe or product, and, most important, an essay describing her Betty-like skills and qualities: cooking and baking, resourcefulness and creativity in everyday tasks, commitment to family and friends, and community involvement.

"We're hoping for an exciting array of nominees," said a spokesperson for General Mills' Betty Crocker Products Division. "Every age, occupation and walk of life is invited." Approximately 210 television and 559 radio stations and 1,500 newspapers reported the multicultural concept behind Betty Crocker's new portrait, a politically correct morphing of white, black, Hispanic, and Asian female faces to reflect the ever changing multicultural mosaic of America. "There's a little bit of Betty Crocker in everyone," General Mills ventured. Or as Russell Adams, the chairman of African-American studies at Howard University in Washington, D.C., told *The Wall Street Journal,* Betty "will be less white bread and more whole-wheat."

Between 4,000 and 5,000 nominations for the Spirit of Betty Crocker arrived at General Mills headquarters, pitting college cheerleaders against great-grandmothers, research scientists against lawyers, teachers, doctors, homemakers, and elected officials for the coveted seventy-five finalist slots. A panel of six women of equally diverse backgrounds selected the winners. "As part of the judging procedure, we weren't allowed to see photos of the women, but could only read their nominations," explained judge Barbara Davis (president of Ken Davis Products, a Minnesota-based food company). One winning essayist proclaimed:

> *For me the phrase "Spirit of Betty Crocker" conjures images of the heavenly aroma of devil's food cake baking in my grandmother's kitchen and me sticky-faced with whatever batter is left on the beaters while my two younger brothers clean the mixing bowl and spatula with grubby little hands. It's me busily chopping pecans in a old wooden bowl and learning how to crack eggs into a cup*

*and dropping them one at time into the dry mix, breathing
in the chocolate dust, then helping my great grandmother
count 300 strokes by hand while she mixes brownie batter
in her favorite blue stoneware bowl.*

The Spirit of Betty Crocker winners ranged in age from
twenty to eighty-three, hailing from thirty-one states and two
Canadian provinces. "I'm happy to be a part of this history," said
a fifty-three-year-old winner, Sandy Work, of Affton, Missouri.
"Fortunately, I look good in red." Sofia Schwarz, of Seattle, said,
"It's so wonderful to see the new portrait and to know that I was
part of the inspiration. Betty Crocker has been a part of my life
for many years and I'm proud to be a part of her today." Among
the winners was a woman whose given name was actually Betty
Crocker—one of seven Betty Crockers to enter the contest.
Prizes included a Betty Crocker red spoon diamond pin, a special copy of Betty Crocker's anniversary cookbook, and a $500
donation to an elementary school of the winner's choice.

Best of all was the permanent spot in Betty history. To create
the Betty Crocker seventy-fifth anniversary portrait, General
Mills commissioned a Florida firm, Lifestyle Software Group, to
digitally blend the facial features of all seventy-five winners with
the 1986 Betty portrait. Each of the seventy-five would receive
1.3 percent representation, less than a person's genetic share in a
newborn great-great-great-grand-child.

The design process—which *The Wall Street Journal* called
"the wildest face lift in the history of American marketing"—took
five graphic artists six weeks to complete. A Minnesota artist,
John Stuart Ingle, had the challenge of transforming this composite into a believable portrait without losing Betty Crocker's
distinct qualities. "Painting the portrait of Betty Crocker was a

Betty Crocker's seventy-fifth anniversary portrait update. The artist, John Stuart Ingle, painted the portrait from a computerized composite of the faces of the seventy-five winners of the Spirit of Betty Crocker contest.

   242

daunting task, but these women and their heartwarming stories truly inspired me," said Ingle. "I've portrayed a woman who is exceptionally knowledgeable, yet imminently approachable and genuinely caring."

On March 19, 1996, the unveiling ceremony was televised live from New York City's Hotel Inter-Continental. Ingle's rendition is the first brown-eyed Betty Crocker. Her eyes have an almond shape and she looks about forty years old, give or take a few years. For the first time since 1955, she is showing some teeth. The new Betty has a Latina look, and her completion is darker, less rosy than the former Bettys'. Her short, no-nonsense hair is dark with ever-so-slight auburn highlights. She wears a red V-neck, button-down cardigan with a white, round-collared blouse underneath. A not-so-subtle gold necklace is in evidence, along with simple gold earrings. One commentator noted that Betty looks like many women dressed in casual Friday attire or to attend her kid's soccer game.

More than 700 newspapers, 460 television stations, and 565 radio stations carried the news of Betty's newfound multiculturalism, which generated 350 million media impressions in just one year. By and large, the 1996 Betty was well received. Several critics did complain that she seemed to be caught in a computer-generated trance; others could not get past the painted window backdrop, which seemed to come directly out of Betty's head. Most of the controversy surrounding Betty's new look rather tamely grazed the surface of deeper issues such as how this exercise in political correctness might have been undertaken merely for the sake of turning a profit. In September 1995, even before the official unveiling, the *Christian Science Monitor* voiced a few mild quibbles—"And while Betty gets a new look, is she holding onto certain ideals of American women . . . that also need updating? . . . Yes"—but ultimately pronounced that Betty can offer "the best of both worlds." Many applauded General Mills' efforts to make Betty Crocker more ethnically inclusive. The historian Ruth Cowan allowed that "to some people," Betty's ethnic portrait "may smack of political correctness, but what it is is responsiveness. This society is dealing with a different racial mix than it has in the past." And the columnist Bill Maxwell of the *St. Petersburg Times* called Betty's seventy-fifth-anniversary portrait "noble," suggesting that Betty Crocker and her African-American counterpart, Aunt Jemima, could be tablemates in an ambassadorship of culinary and cultural goodwill.

However, Betty's "everywoman portrait" did touch off one overarching debate, which stemmed from General Mills' claim that she represents a diverse market. Critics cried foul, citing the exclusion of men who use Betty Crocker's products and recipes. Tepid charges of sexism inevitably led to suggestions that the next portrait update should morph men's faces into Betty Crocker, giving Betty an androgynous look. Fortunately, most critics conceded that a she-male Betty Crocker was no solution. Some journalists campaigned for a male sidekick for Betty—Bob Crocker. But what chance does Bob Crocker have in a realm traditionally dominated by women? Ultimately, these skirmishes underscore Betty Crocker's most human limitation: she cannot possibly be all things to all people.

Despite the great challenge of reflecting the scope of a national market in one woman's portrait, the corporate vision for Betty headed straight and strong into the new millennium. Soon after the unveiling of Betty's 1996 portrait, she made a comeback on many packaged food items. Her face also appears on her interactive website, in cookbooks and recipe booklets and in many newspapers that run her syndicated column, *Ask Betty*. Visitors

   244

to Betty's home state can catch a glimpse of her at special events sponsored by Betty Crocker Kitchens or spot her every August when she smiles from the rafters above the Betty Crocker Kitchens' demonstration booth at the Minnesota State Fair. In 2001, an entire ballpark of minor league baseball fans received a Betty mask on a stick, celebrating Betty Crocker Day at a St. Paul Saints game. And a permanent exhibit at the Minnesota Historical Society's Mill City Museum pays homage to their hometown girl. All roads in Minnesota do not lead to Betty, but many do lead to Betty Crocker Drive.

Notes

Chapter One: The Making of an American Myth

9   "Why does my cake fall?": See James Gray, *Business Without Boundary: The Story of General Mills* (Minneapolis: University of Minnesota Press, 1954), p. 172.

11   "Betty" sounded cheery, wholesome, and folksy: Ibid., p. 173; General Mills, "Betty Crocker . . . 1921–1954" (Minneapolis, privately printed, c. 1954) p. 2; Norman Carlisle, "The Amazing Lady Who Ran Away With a Company," *Cornet*, December 1954, p. 143. Note: As far as creation myths go, Betty Crocker's is legendary—with at least a handful of people taking credit for it. Consequently, there are several versions of Betty's origins. Gray's, et al, versions are the most widely recognized and probable version of Betty Crocker's creation.

11   "The winner was a secretary named Florence Lindeberg": Gray, p. 174.

12   those "big, shiny pieces": "History of Housework," transcript of Susan Stamberg interview of Susan Strasser, *Morning Edition*, National Public Radio, August 24, 2004.

14   "sauces . . . even mayonnaise!": General Mills Inc., *Gold Medal Flour Cook Book* (Minneapolis: Washburn Crosby Co., Reprint, 1983), from the Preface.

14 Lydia E. Pinkham: See Juliann Sivulka, *Soap, Sex, and Cigarettes: A Cultural History of American Advertising* (Belmont, California: Wadsworth Publishing, 1997), p. 39.

14 women controlled 80 to 85 percent of consumer spending: See Roland Marchand, *Advertising the American Dream: Making Way for Modernity 1920–1940* (Berkeley: University of California Press, 1986), p. 66.

14–16 "At Miss Farmer's Famous": *McCall's*, February 1926, p. 78.

16 "apprenticeship of the stove": Gray, p. 178.

16 approaching 106 million: http://www.census.gov, Appendix A, United States' population and Census Cost.

16 on meat, vegetables, eggs, and flour: *Ladies' Home Journal*, May 1925, p. 139.

17 "Pour a little Pillsbury's Pancake Flour": *Ladies' Home Journal*, February 1924, p. 70.

17 Swans Down brand: *Ladies' Home Journal*, October 1924, p. 104.

17 "finest wheat": *Ladies' Home Journal*, April 1925, p. 137.

17 "Aunt Jemima Pancakes": *Ladies' Home Journal*, January 1924, p. 111.

17 "Aunt Jemima didn't use ordinary flour": *Ladies' Home Journal*, March 1924, p. 145.

17 "Gold Medal Label": *McCall's*, October 1926, p. 26.

17 "Unqualified Guarantee": *Ladies' Home Journal*, September 1925, p. 216.

19 "Pillsbury's Best Flour": *McCall's*, October 1926, p. 91.

19 "Why pay more?": *McCall's*, October 1926, p. 26.

19 "Miss Betty Crocker and her staff": *Ladies' Home Journal*, September 1925, p. 216.

19 "neat wooden box": *McCall's*, April 1926, p. 37.

20 "for only $1.00": *McCall's,* November 1926, p. 53.

20 "my biscuits are wonderful dainties": Gold Medal Flour magazine advertisement, 1927, General Mills Archives.

22 Home economists Ina Rowe: Gray, pp. 171, 175–77.

22 "faint suggestion of sogginess": Washburn Crosby Company, *What Every Woman Should Know About Baking: The New Meaning of Flour—by Betty Crocker* (Minneapolis: Washburn Crosby Co., 1926), p. 2.

22 auditoriums filled to capacity: General Mills, oral history of Marjorie Child Husted, conducted by Jean Tell, July 26, 1985; *The Eventually News,* August 1, 1923.

22 borrowed electric stove: Ibid.

25 "art of camp cookery": General Mills, *The Eventually News,* September 13, 1922.

26 "Science in Your Oven": *Ladies' Home Journal,* May 1924, p. 145.

26 "recipe you'd love to prepare": General Mills, Inc. *Gold Medal Flour Cook Book* (Minneapolis: Washburn Crosby Co., reprint, 1983), preface.

26 "Times certainly have changed": Ibid.

26 "at about $900": Bunny Crumpacker, *The Old-Time Brand Name Cookbook: Recipes, Illustrations, and Advice from the Early Kitchens of America's Most Trusted Food Makers* (New York: Smithmark, 1998), p. xiv.

26 "Electrical equipment": *McCall's,* June 1927, p. 37.

26 "Up-to-Date Kitchen League": *McCall's,* June 1926, p. 38.

27 "Westinghouse Electrical Appliances": *Ladies' Home Journal,* February 1925, p. 170.

27 "The Kitchen is the cheapest": *Ladies' Home Journal,* April 1924, p. 84.

27 "more than ninety-five": *McCall's,* June 1927, p. 37.

28   Fannie Farmer had to pay: http://www.foodreference.com.

28   "that remorseless demand": *Ladies' Home Journal*, May 1924, p. 86.

29   radio ownership soared 2.5 million: http://www.rca.com.

29   National Broadcasting Company: Ibid.

29   topped out at 30 million: Ibid.

29   its nearest competitor: *Ladies' Home Journal*, January 1925, p. 134.

30   "voices are *real*": Ibid., p. 100.

30   "The radio made Betty": General Mills of Minneapolis, *Fortune*, April 1945, p. 117.

30   Blanche Ingersoll introduced herself: Gray, p. 176.

30   "Good morning": Betty Crocker Radio Script, October 2, 1924, General Mills Archives.

31   People's Gas Company: History of Betty Crocker, General Mills internal document, n.p., n.d., General Mills Archives.

31   "If you load a man's": Betty Crocker Radio Script, October 2, 1924, General Mills Archives.

31   "she has the wrong point of view": Ibid.

32   "it may be that you are a young housekeeper": Ibid.

32   "Gold Medal Radio Station": *McCall's*, October 1926, p. 91.

35   *Betty Crocker's Cooking School of the Air*: General Mills, "Betty Crocker . . . 1921–1954" (Minneapolis, privately printed, c. 1954), Appendix "a."

36   "make the humdrum exciting": Excerpts from letters sent to Betty Crocker, 1920s–1930s, General Mills Archives.

36   "And the men—indeed I have not forgotten the men": Betty Crocker Radio Script, January 20, 1926. General Mills Archives.

37   twelve regional stations: Betty Crocker Radio Script, September 21, 1925, General Mills Archives.

37 "Won't it be fun": Betty Crocker Radio Script, October 5, 1927, General Mills Archives.

38 "making history this morning": Betty Crocker Radio Script, January 20, 1926, General Mills Archives.

38 Each week, "tens of thousands" of letters: Gray, p. 177.

38 "I am a young bride wanting so much to do things right in cooking": Excerpt from letter sent to Betty Crocker, 1920s–1930s, General Mills Archives.

39 Marjorie Child Husted: Gray, p. 175.

41 "I like to picture you as I talk": Betty Crocker Radio Script, October 5, 1927, General Mills Archives.

41 Marjorie Child Husted was not exactly Betty personified: Gray, p. 175; Marjorie Child Husted's unfinished autobiography, Child Family Collection; Carol Pine, "The Real Betty Crocker is One Tough Cookie," *Twin Cities*, November 1978, p. 46; General Mills, oral history of Marjorie Child Husted, conducted by Jean Toll, July 26, 1985.

41 Under Husted's direction, Betty Crocker's cooking shows: General Mills, "Betty Crocker . . . 1921–1954" (Minneapolis, privately printed, c. 1954), pp. 3–5. Note: Throughout Betty Crocker's thirty-plus years on the radio, her programs also aired on CBS and ABC networks, depending on contractual agreements and individual stations.

42 "Please don't let me do all the planning": Betty Crocker Radio Script, October 5, 1927, General Mills Archives.

42 "danger of her capturing my husband?": Excerpt from letter sent to Betty Crocker, 1920s–1930s, General Mills Archives.

43 "And now in closing": Betty Crocker Radio Script, April 1, 1927, General Mills Archives.

Chapter Two: Betty Goes Hollywood

49   NBC network, several mornings a week: *Ladies' Home Journal,* January 1930, p. 146.

49   radio advertising dollars reached 31 million: http://www.media history.umn.edu/time.

49   "The radio, it seems to me": Christine Frederick, "A Real Use for Radio," *Good Housekeeping,* July 1922, p. 77.

49   Model Kitchen of H. J. Heinz Company: *Ladies' Home Journal,* February 1930, p. 133.

50   "Yo-Ho! Ho-Yo!": *Ladies' Home Journal,* March 1930, p. 166.

50   "Aunt Jemima . . . the Quaker Man": *Ladies' Home Journal,* October 1930, p. 50.

50   "don't miss the coast to coast": *Ladies' Home Journal,* November 1930, p. 59.

50   "Tune in on General Foods Baking Day": *McCall's,* April 1933, p. 58.

51   By 1933, around 250,000 on-air students registered for her *Cooking School of the Air:* General Mills, "Betty Crocker . . . 1921–1954" (Minneapolis, privately printed, c. 1954), Appendix "a."

51   close to 30 percent of a labor force: Russell Nixon and Paul Samuelson, "Estimates of Unemployment in the United States," *Reviews of Economic Statistics* 22 (August 1940), pp. 106–7; cited in Harvey Levenstein, *Paradox of Plenty: A Social History of Eating in Modern America* (New York: Oxford University Press, 1993), p. 4.

51   population of 122 million: Dr. William M. Steuart, Director, U.S. Bureau of Census, United States Census, 1930.

51   "Kindly send me a copy": Excerpts from letters sent to Betty Crocker, 1920s–1930s, General Mills Archives.

52 "United States spends thirty per cent for food": *Ladies' Home Journal,* December 1930, p. 24.

52 "Miss Crocker, sometimes I become so discouraged": Excerpts from letters sent to Betty Crocker, 1920s–1930s, General Mills Archives.

53 Roosevelts during the Depression: Morris Markey, "Dear Mr. Roosevelt—The Inside Story of the President's Correspondences," *McCall's,* May 1934, p. 4.

53 "Fireside Chats": *McCall's,* September 1933, p. 14.

53 "Your talks have a real person-to-person feeling": Excerpt from letters sent to Betty Crocker, 1920s–1930s, General Mills Archives.

53 two of Betty's weekly broadcasts: *Good Housekeeping,* January 1935, p. 147.

54 "Thrift has always been the banner of house-wifely skill": Betty Crocker Radio Script, June 1, 1932, General Mills Archives.

54 "universal three meals a day": Lita Bane, "The Modern Home-maker," *Ladies' Home Journal,* February 1930, p. 100.

54 "Your talks, Betty Crocker, have given me hope": Excerpts from letters sent to Betty Crocker, 1920s–1930s, General Mills Archives.

56 "Now we live on a budget and far more economical": Ibid.

56 "You see Betty Crocker, I am a blind girl": Ibid.

57 "I had to settle for the name of Teddy": Ibid.

57 "It should be pointed out, as a comment on the character of Betty Crocker": Gray, *Business Without Boundary,* pp. 179–80.

57 "Would you serve this in your own home?": Series of oral history interviews with Ruby Peterson, former Betty Crocker staffer, conducted by Susan Marks, 1999–2000.

58 "My wife is the greatest cook in the world": *McCall's,* January 1933, back cover.

60 created Bisquick: Beverly Bundy, *The Century in Food: America's Fads and Favorites* (Portland, Oregon: Collector's Press, 2002), p. 91.

60 "look for a kiss and a compliment from your husband": *McCall's*, September 1933, inside front cover.

60 "sensation at the luncheon or tea table": Dorothy Kirk, "Waffles," *McCall's*, January 1933, p. 50.

60 "magic of Betty Crocker can make them": *McCall's*, December 1934, back cover.

60 "Family size—makes 80 Bisquicks": *McCall's*, December 1934, back cover.

61 "So why bake when you can *buy* cake": *Ladies' Home Journal*, February 1930, p. 143.

61 "Don't say you can't win": *McCall's*, December 1933, back cover.

61 "Now this is no ordinary contest": Betty Crocker Radio Script, December 3, 1933, General Mills Archives.

63 "Not So Dumb": Betty Crocker Radio Script, October 12, 1938. General Mills Archives.

64 "I want you to know": Excerpts from letters sent to Betty Crocker, 1920s–1930s, General Mills Archives.

66 "whether or not she can cook!": Ibid.

67 "I am doing lots better in many things": Ibid.

67 "The Girl the Football Hero Is Looking For": General Mills internal document, Preparation of Radio Broadcasts by Husted, 1937; General Mills internal document, "Proposed Schedule of Betty Crocker Radio Talks," September 18, 1931, General Mills Archives.

67 "I think he has the right idea": Excerpts from letters sent to Betty Crocker, 1920s–1930s, General Mills Archives.

69 "you have my opinion on the matter": Ibid.

70 "appealed to me that I just could not refrain": Ibid.

70 "they were eager for a wife who could cook": Husted unfinished autobiography.

70 "I will get you a hubby yet!": General Mills internal memo attached to letter sent to Betty Crocker, c. 1930s, General Mills Archives.

72 "I am helping you with your housekeeping problems": Betty Crocker Radio Script, October 1, 1929, General Mills Archives.

72 "Perhaps one of the real blessings": "Mrs. Roosevelt Replies to the Letter of an Unknown Woman," *McCall's*, March 1933, p. 4.

72 "60 million to 80 million Americans attended the movies each week": http://www.digitalhistory.uh.edu/historyonline/hollywood.

73 "Joan Crawford—who, not unlike Betty": General Mills, *Take a Trick a Day with Bisquick—Let the Stars Show You How* (Minneapolis: General Mills, Inc., 1935), and *Betty Crocker's 101 Delicious Bisquick Creations* (Minneapolis: General Mills, Inc., 1933), p. 16.

73 Husted as Betty irresistible: Husted unfinished autobiography; Husted oral history interview by Toll.

73 "Question Box": Betty Crocker Radio Script, November 11, 1936, General Mills Archives.

77 "that will be favorites with the men": Betty Crocker Radio Script, March 1, 1937, General Mills Archives.

77 Robert Taylor "didn't feel competent to talk about women": Ibid.

77 "The Clark Gable frosting sounded very intriguing": Excerpt from letter sent to Betty Crocker, 1920s–1930s, General Mills Archives.

78 "I love bread—always have it in some form, three times a day": *Vitality Demands Energy: 109 Smart Ways to Serve Bread—Our Outstanding Energy Food* (Minneapolis: General Mills, Inc., 1934), p. 35.

78 "people afraid of white-flour bread": Levenstein, p. 15.

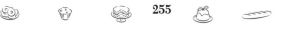

81   "smart luminaries of movieland": General Mills, *Trick a Day*,
      front cover.

81   sweet potatoes, and chocolate icebox cake: Ibid., pp. 13, 16, 25.

81   Husted's Hollywood personification of Betty Crocker: Husted
      unfinished autobiography.

82   "nothing more important than bringing up children!": Betty
      Crocker Radio Script, November 9, 1936, General Mills Archives.

82   A 1940 national survey: "Star of Stars," Attitude survey conducted
      for General Mills, 1940, Summary, General Mills Archives.

82   "Golden Eight": James Gray, General Mills, "General Mills—An
      Idea in Action," *Horizons*, Spring 1953, p. 6.

Chapter Three: On Betty's Watch

87   foods for building strong bodies, steady nerves, and high morale:
      McCall's, September 1942, pp. 48–49.

87   President Roosevelt told American women: *McCall's*, February
      1942, pp. 16–17.

87   "men at sea, men in tanks, men with guns": *McCall's*, February
      1942, pp. 16–17.

87   The U.S. government's "Consumer Pledge": *McCall's*, February
      1942, pp. 16–17.

87   abundance of consumables: *Ladies' Home Journal*, August 1941.

88   "sugar book": Joanne Lamb Hayes, *Grandma's Wartime Baking
      Book: World War II and the Way We Baked* (New York: St.
      Martin's Press, 2003), p. xv.

88   The weekly allowance: Levenstein, *Paradox of Plenty*, p. 80.

88   Coffee, butter: Hayes, *Grandma's Wartime Baking Book*, p. xv.

88   "Let's make rationing work!": *Ladies' Home Journal*, May 1943,
      p. 75.

88–91   "Use corn syrup to sweeten the whipped cream": *McCall's,* July 1942, p. 52.

91   "gladden hearts, save sugar": *McCall's,* February 1943, p. 78.

91   "Of course! Simple to make": *McCall's,* November 1942, p. 68.

91   "Make it do. Or do without": Joanne Lamb Hayes, *Grandma's Wartime Kitchen: World War II and the Way We Cooked* (New York: St. Martin's Press, 2000), p. 5.

91   launching of a single big ship required: *McCall's,* July 1943, p. 8.

91   "or clarified drippings may be used": General Mills, *Your Share: How to prepare appetizing, healthful meals with foods available today by Betty Crocker,* 1943, p. 15.

92   "1,000,000 loaves a year": *McCall's,* August 1943, p. 7.

92   "Save your 'blue' stamps": General Mills, *Your Share,* p. 22.

92   "cupcakes for dessert": *McCall's,* June 1943, p. 89.

92   "It's good to extend your meat with Wheaties": *McCall's,* April 1943, p. 90.

92   Emergency Steak: *McCall's,* March 1943, p. 91; *Your Share,* p. 7.

93   "Better breakfasts are in order!": *McCall's,* May 1943, p. 83.

94   "I wasted no food this day": General Mills, *Your Share,* p. 37.

94   Victory Lunch Box Meal: General Mills, *War-Time Services for the Home-Front,* bulletin IV, n.p., n.d.

94   "an attractive flower decoration": General Mills, *Your Share,* pp. 31–35, 43.

94   fortification of milk and flour: Levenstein, p. 69.

94   Gold Medal Flour as "Vitamin-Mineral Enriched": *McCall's,* September 1942, back cover.

94   carry the AMA label of "preferred" food: "All Gold Medal is vitamin and mineral enriched. Thus it's a 'preferred' food." Gold Medal Flour advertisement, 1942, cited in Hayes, *Grandma's Wartime Baking Book,* p. 109.

99 "made the Betty Crocker way": *McCall's,* September 1942, back cover.

99 Doughboy's Special: General Mills, *War-time Services for the Home-Front,* bulletin, n.d.,n.p.

99 "that boy in the service": McCall's, December 1942, p. 58.

100 "Cordially, Betty Crocker": Except from Betty Crocker letter reply, 1940s, General Mills Archives.

101 "job in a defense plant to help end this thing": Excerpt from letters sent to Betty Crocker, 1940s, General Mills Archives.

104 "working long hard hours to cover them all": Betty Crocker Radio Script, November 3, 1944, General Mills Archives.

104 Legionnaires were eligible for prizes: General Mills' internal document, *The War Comes to Betty Crocker,* n.d., n.p; General Mills, *Homemaker Report to Betty Crocker—Home Legion,* n.d., n.p., General Mills Archives.

105 "You must be a grand person": Excerpts from letters sent to Betty Crocker, 1940s, General Mills Archives.

106 "you boost my morale 100% whenever I hear you": Ibid.

106 "ever been done for the American homemaker": General Mills, "Outline of the Career in Advertising of Marjorie Child Husted," February 1950, General Mills Archives.

108 "in these simple, inglorious tasks": Betty Crocker Radio Script, March 14, 1945, General Mills Archives.

111 the Pillsbury Bake-Off: Unpublished manuscript of one of Leo Burnett's original founders, Dewitt Jack O'Kieffe, c. 1970s, Leo Burnett Archives.

114 Eleanor Roosevelt championed the Bake-Off: Bundy, *The Century in Food,* p. 111.

114 rounded out the top four, at 2.7 percent: General Mills' Betty Crocker Attitude Survey, "The Most Helpful Home Economics Personality," 1949, General Mills Archives.

114 4,000 to 5,000 letters *daily*: General Mills, oral history of Mar-
jorie Child Husted, conducted by Jean Toll, July 26, 1985, p. 36;
Gray, *Business Without Boundary*, p. 178; General Mills' "Betty
Crocker Chronology," 1948, pp. 7–9; *General Mills: 75 Years of
Innovation, Invention, Food and Fun*, General Mills private pub-
lication, 2003, p. 26.

114 Mary Margaret McBride: See Michele Hilmes, *Radio Voices:
American Broadcasting, 1922–1952* (Minneapolis: University of
Minnesota Press, 1997), p. 279.

116 nine out of ten homes: General Mills' Betty Crocker Attitude
Survey, 1949, General Mills Archives.

116 "$1 on the General Mills accounting books": *Fortune*, 1945, pp.
116–17.

119 "biggest morale job in history": See Loren Baritz, *The Good Life:
The Meaning of Success for the American Middle Class*, cited in
Levenstein, *Paradox of Plenty*, p. 102.

119 "the problem without a name": See Betty Friedan's *The Feminine
Mystique* (New York: Dell Publishing, 1984), p. 15.

119 Take pride in your homemaking skills: General Mills, *Rules for
Better Home Management*, "A Homemaker's Dozen," 1946; General Mills, *Betty Crocker's Home Management for Happiness*,
1946, General Mills Archives.

120 "a place of peace, joy and contentment": General Mills, *Betty
Crocker's Home Management for Happiness*.

120 "happiness for yourself and your dear ones": Ibid.

121 "copied this habit of mine": Ibid.

121 "these same maturing experiences": Betty Crocker Radio Script,
January 15, 1946, General Mills Archives.

121 "run a mighty poor second to a talent for cooking": *Ladies' Home
Journal*, March 1942, p. 41.

121 "what a G.I. dreams of! Lady—make his dreams come true!":

Crisco advertisement, January 1946. Cited in Hayes, *Grandma's Wartime Baking Book*, p. 63.

121 "Young Mother": Letter sent to Betty Crocker, January 1946, General Mills Archives.

123 "you should not still be the best of sweethearts": Letters sent to Betty Crocker in response to "Young Mother," January 1946, General Mills Archives.

125 "Now if I can only prove myself worthy": Letter from "Young Mother" sent to Betty Crocker, February 1946, General Mills Archives.

126 "to remind them that they had value": Carol Pine, "The Real Betty Crocker is One Tough Cookie," *Twin Cities*, November 1978, p. 46.

Chapter Four: Bake Someone Happy

131 In a "kitchen just like yours": *McCall's*, November 1926, p. 53.

131 "cook book full of [Betty's] famous tested recipes": *Betty Crocker Picture Cook Book*, foreword by Betty Crocker, 1950.

131 *Betty Crocker's Cook Book of All Purpose Baking: McCall's*, October 1942, p. 71, and *McCall's*, November 1942, p. 95.

131 *Big Red* is in its ninth edition and has sold more than 30 million: General Mills Public Relations e-mail, April 5, 2004.

133 Husted became: General Mills internal document, History of Betty Crocker, General Mills Archives, c. 1962.

133 "lots of 'em in gorgeous color": Betty Crocker Radio Script, September 8, 1950, General Mills Archives.

134 "At last A Betty Crocker Cook Book.": *Ladies' Home Journal*, November 1950.

134 the gift of choice at bridal showers: See Karal Ann Marling, *As Seen on TV: The Visual Culture of Everyday Life in the 1950s*

(Cambridge, Massachusetts: Harvard University Press, 1994), p. 203.

134 the Bible for the top spot: General Mills internal company newsletter, *Modern Millwheel*, January 1951; *Modern Millwheel*, November 1953.

134 complimentary copy: http://www.meredith.com.

134 15 million copies by 1996: http://www.mediahistory.umn.edu/time/1930s.html.

134 between 1951 and 1958: See Anne Mendelson, *Stand Facing the Stove: The Story of the Women Who Gave America the Joy of Cooking®* (New York: Henry Holt & Company, 1996), p. 279.

134 The press was more than kind to Betty: *Modern Millwheel*, January 1951.

136 Dear Friend: *Betty Crocker's Picture Cook Book (Big Red)* (New York: McGraw-Hill, 1950), introduction, p. 5.

136 "Please try my mother's recipe": Ibid., p. 65.

138 "Don't miss the recipes marked": Ibid., introduction, p. 5.

138 "We call it our vitamin dessert": *McCall's*, March 1943, p. 58.

138 "Surprise! Guess what's in it! Moist, goozly!": *Big Red*, p. 221.

138 "'gentle art' of cake making": Ibid., p. 117.

139 "modern way": Ibid., pp. 120–21.

139 "Well, we have": Ibid., pp. 120–60.

139 "Elegant Cake Desserts": Ibid., pp. 209–48.

139 "A butter icing is like": Ibid., p. 161.

140 "What month is your birth date?": Ibid., p. 165.

140 "cake and give to women guests": Ibid.

140 "present with a kiss hug": Ibid.

141 "recipe from France in 1790": Ibid., p. 248.

141 "an inspiration to us all": Ibid.

141 "Pure white heavenly concoction": Ibid., p. 321.

141 one of Betty's home recipe testers: Ibid., p. 155.

141 "our own Vice President": Ibid., p. 134.

141 "Their shells should look dull": Ibid., p. 250.

141 "'Cooky Shines'?": Ibid., p. 175.

142 His Mother's Oatmeal Cookies: Ibid., p. 174.

143 "vegetables in disguise!": Ibid., p. 414.

143 "Smart homemakers say: 'My meals are more interesting'": Ibid., p. 34.

143 "Cortez the Spanish conquistador": Ibid., p. 56.

143 "good coffee is an asset": Ibid., p. 54.

144 "Hush, puppies!": Ibid., p. 71.

144 "Let your head save your heels": Ibid., pp. 427–34.

144 "Get a medical check-up": Ibid.

147 "complete assurance and success": Ibid., p. 432.

147 "the happy ending we've anticipated from the very first": Ibid., p. 209.

147 $100 million in Betty Crocker: Levenstein, *Paradox of Plenty*, p. 115.

147 "the most trusted friend in the kitchen": *Betty Crocker's Picture Cook Book*, foreword to the 2002 facsimile edition.

Chapter Five: Just Add Water!

153 "But now I am really proud of the ones I make": Excerpt from letter sent to Betty Crocker, 1920s–1930s, General Mills Archives.

153 "Cakes have become the very symbol": General Mills, *Betty Crocker Cook Book of All-Purpose Cooking*, 1942, p. 10.

153 than a billion cakes: See Karal Ann Marling, *As Seen on TV*, p. 228.

154 "there's nothing like a home-baked cake": *Betty Crocker's Ulti-*

mate Cake Mix Cookbook (Hoboken, New Jersey: John Wiley & Sons, Inc., 2004), foreword.

154   "There is something about a good cake": Gold Medal Flour magazine advertisement, 1922, General Mills Archives.

154   "I recommend that you try": Betty Crocker Radio Script, c. 1930, General Mills Archives.

156   "spoiled the day for both of them!": General Mills, *New Party Cakes for All Occasions* (Minneapolis: Gold Medal Foods, 1931), pp. 3–4.

156   "Cake Clinics": Betty Crocker Radio Script, September 4, 1935, General Mills Archives.

157   "ideal dessert for St. Valentine's Day": Ibid., pp. 1–24.

158   "guesswork is taken out of it!": Betty Crocker Radio Script, October 13, 1944, General Mills Archives.

158   Promotions for Double-Quick: General Mills press release, September 22, 1947.

158   *carefree* baking days once more: Gold Medal Flour magazine advertisement, 1946, General Mills Archives.

161   own mini baking revolution: Mary Hart, "Mystery Cake, Secret 'Ingredient X' Revealed for Baking Mammoth 'Chiffon,'" *Minneapolis Star and Tribune*, 1948; General Mills, "New Chiffon Cake Makes News," 1948, General Mills Archives.

163   "dry as some are prone to be": General Mills' internal publication, "Read Your Future in a Cake," *Horizons*, March 1948; "New Chiffon Cake Makes News."

163   "Dear Betty Crocker": Letter sent to Betty Crocker, February 25, 1948, General Mills Archives.

164   By 1952, the average U.S. grocery: See Bundy, *The Century in Food*, p. 113.

166   cake mixes before World War II: General Mills internal docu-

ment, "The History of Betty Crocker's Cake Mixes," May 31, 1955; General Mills internal document, "Some Notes on Flour Mix History," June 8, 1954; General Mills internal document, "History of Cake Mixes," September 1, 1972.

166 more popular: Candy Sagon, "In Praise of the Perfect Pan," *The Washington Post*, November 13, 2002.

167 men preferred blue: Levenstein, *Paradox of Plenty*, p. 115.

167 introduce a chocolate cake mix: "A Range of Endeavors: General Mills and Its Various Ancestors Have Tried Their Hands at a Lot of Things Over the Years, Developing Some Interesting 'Firsts' in the Process," *Minneapolis Star Tribune*, June 18, 2003.

168 captured a 48 percent share: Bundy, p. 115.

168 Chocolate Malt (1955): General Mills, *Betty Crocker's Ultimate Cake Mix Cookbook*, p. 7.

168 cake mix . . . cheapened that love: Marling, pp. 212–13, 224–31.

170 novel invention at the White House: Ibid., p. 228.

170 Betty Crocker, once again, reigned supreme: Betty Crocker cake mix magazine advertisement, 1952, General Mills Archives.

170 use of mixes increased 343 percent: General Mills internal publication, "Batter up!," *Horizons*, February 1952, pp. 16–17.

171 rifle through the kitchen trash: Oral history interview with Ruby Peterson; oral history interview with Ruth Springer, conducted by Susan Marks, January 1999.

171 "Let's have a pink party": Betty Crocker cake mix magazine advertisement, n.d., General Mills Archives.

173 "Honey Spice Cake Mix": Ibid.

173 "Kenner's Easy-Bake® Oven": See David Hoffman, *The Easy-Bake® Oven Gourmet* (Philadelphia: Running Press Book Publishers, 2003), p. 26.

175 "60 percent of households": Sylvia Carter, "Mix it Up: The Devil's Food Made Us Do It," *Newsday*, September 23, 1998.

175 "cake from scratch again": Christine Arpe Gang, "General Mills Whoops It Up for Betty Crocker's 50th Anniversary," *The Commercial Appeal* (Memphis, TN), September 16, 1998.

Chapter Six: Kitchens of the World

181 At least 2 million tourists: General Mills Public Relation's material, "The Story of Betty Crocker," n.d., n.p.

181 impossible to meet Betty Crocker: Peterson oral history.

183 model kitchen boasted gas and electric ranges: Washburn Crosby Company internal newsletter, *The Eventually News*, September 1924, p. 12.

183 "the new art of living electrically": General Electric publication, "The New Art of Buying, Preserving and Preparing Foods," 1934.

183 Campbell's Soup Home Economics Kitchen: Campbell's publication, "Easy Ways to Good Meals: 99 Delicious Dishes Made with Campbell's Soups," c. 1941, p. 48.

183 H. J. Heinz Company: H. J. Heinz Co., "The Heinz Book of Salads," c. 1930, p. 91.

184 "Celebrating Our Tenth Anniversary in a New Home": Betty Crocker Radio Script, October 3, 1934, General Mills Archives.

187 "The Tasting Test": Betty Crocker Radio Script, October 5, 1934, General Mills Archives.

187 Mary Hale Martin for Libby's: Libby, McNeill & Libby, *My Best Recipes*, c. 1934.

191 But at Betty's table, innovations in market research: Betty Crocker Radio Script, October 5, 1934, General Mills Archives.

191 Betty's "famous tested recipes": General Mills' sales material, "General Mills' Betty Crocker: Overwhelmingly voted by American Homemakers the most helpful home service personality," c. 1947, General Mills Archives.

191   Did you like the recipe?: Ibid.

192   Triple-Testing: Ibid.

192   Betty Crocker Kitchens: General Mills internal document, "Betty
Crocker Guide to the New Home Service Department at Gen-
eral Mills," 1947, General Mills Archives; General Mills press
release, "Happy Birthday, Betty Crocker: Betty Crocker and
How She Grew, A Brief History of the Betty Crocker Food and
Publications Center," June 1991; General Mills' Betty Crocker
Kitchen Tour Brochure, "Welcome to the home of Betty Crocker,"
n.d., n.p.

192–93   cubbyholes stored personal items: "Betty Crocker Guide to
the New Home Service Department at General Mills," 1947,
General Mills Archives.

193   Betty's extensive library of cookbooks: Ibid.

193   "hum of activity": General Mills' Betty Crocker Kitchen Tour
Brochure, "Welcome to the home of Betty Crocker," n.d., n.p.

193   a glimpse of Betty's secrets: "Betty Crocker Guide to the New
Home Service Department at General Mills," 1947.

193   Kitchen of Tomorrow, two kitchens in one: Ibid.

195   The Kamera Kitchen: Ibid.

195   Polka Dot Kitchen: Ibid.

195   "surprising contrast to the up-to-the-minute kitchens": Ibid.

196   26,519 visitors signed the guest book: General Mills internal document, "History of Betty Crocker," n.d., n.p., General Mills
Archives.

196   *billion* copies of Betty Crocker's tested recipes: General Mills
sales material, "How will Betty Crocker help appliance dealers
and distributors?" c. 1948, General Mills Archives.

196   "Come into our kitchen and see how we test": General Mills'
Betty Crocker Kitchen tour brochure, c. 1955; General Mills'

Betty Crocker Kitchen tour information packet, "News from the Betty Crocker Kitchens," c. 1955.

196   about 10,000 a month: "History of Betty Crocker," n.d., n.p.

198   America's $73 billion food industry: *Life*, January 1959.

198   Trade and Cultural Fair in Moscow: General Mills internal publication, "Betty Crocker Goes to Moscow," *Horizons*, 1959.

198   "Kitchen Debate": *The New York Times*, July 25, 1959.

199   "Follow the Red Spoons": General Mills Annual Report, "Betty Crocker's New Kitchens of the World, May 31, 1965–May 29, 1966; "Happy Birthday, Betty Crocker: Betty Crocker and How She Grew, A Brief History of the Betty Crocker Food and Publications Center," June 1991, General Mills' Betty Crocker Kitchen Tour information packet, "Welcome to the Betty Crocker Kitchens," 1966; General Mills internal document, "Kitchen's Décor as described by Nathan Mandelbaum, Interior Decorator, *Ladies' Home Journal*," c. 1968, General Mills Archives.

199   Mediterranean Kitchen: "Welcome to the Betty Crocker Kitchens," 1966.

199   "Kitchen of the Sun": Ibid.

200   "touch of Oriental beauty": Ibid.

200   The Betty Crocker Kitchens closed: General Mills press release, "Public Tours of Betty Crocker Kitchens will end January 15, 1985," October 19, 1984.

202   "But Betty Crocker is mother": Sylvia Paine, "Bye Bye Betty," *Mpls-St Paul*, January 1985.

202   "Reports from the few people I know": Ibid.

202   "It smelled heavenly—chocolate, baked goods": "She's Part of the New Recipe for A Diverse Betty Crocker," *The Orange County Register*, February 20, 1998.

203   completely new kitchen facility: Rick Nelson, "Betty Crocker fi-

nally gets a new home," *Minneapolis Star Tribune,* October 23, 2003.

203 test 50,000 recipes a year: Ibid.

205 America's largest corporate cookbook library: Ibid.

205 blue panel to represent Pillsbury: Ibid.

Chapter Seven: Strangely Familiar

211 requests for her photograph: General Mills internal radio document—form letter responses: "I am sorry that I must refuse, but the truth is that I simply never have my picture taken. I don't know whether it is because I just naturally don't like to sit and pose or whether it is the disappointment I feel sure would follow, but the fact remains that I haven't had my picture taken for years. I'm sorry," n.d., n.p., General Mills Archives.

212 McMein and the famous dancer Irene Castle: Irene Castle and Neysa McMain, "Ought Mothers Give up Careers for Babies?: Two of the Nation's Most Prominent Mothers Disagree," *McCall's,* February 1926, pp. 17, 111.

215 "Neysa McMein, famous magazine cover artist": General Mills recipe booklet, "Betty Crocker's 15th Prize Recipes: favorite of each year—1921 to 1936."

218 "perfect composite of the twentieth-century American woman": Gray, *Business Without Boundary,* p. 174.

218 "You look exactly like I thought you would!": "History of Betty Crocker," n.p., n.d.

218 "an ageless 32": Jean Libman Block, "The Secret Life of Betty Crocker," *Women's Home Journal,* December 1954.

219 600 percent that year—to a total of 2 million sets: http://www.tvhistory.com.

219 the guy who fought for Betty Crocker: "Retired General Mills Executive, Ad Pioneer James Fish Dies at 82," *Minneapolis Star Tribune,* July 7, 1998.

219 Hawley, for example, was "stunningly blonde": Marling, *As Seen on TV,* p. 211.

219 "a dream in her eyes all women will be quick to recognize": General Mills internal document, "Betty Crocker on Television," n.p., n.d., General Mills Archives.

219 Hawley told the press: "TV's Original Betty Crocker, Adelaide Hawley Cumming, Dead at 93," *Associated Press,* December 24, 1998.

219 *Time for Betty Crocker:* Ibid.; General Mills internal document, "Betty Crocker on Television."

221 "I don't know how to bake a cake, Gracie, but here is Betty Crocker to show us how": "TV's Original Betty Crocker, Adelaide Hawley Cumming, Dead at 93."

221 in 1950, 8 million American homes had sets; in 1958, the figure was 41 million: http://www.tvhistory.com.

221 "broadcasting pioneer and probably the most visible Betty": "First TV Betty Crocker Dies at 93," *The Colombian,* December 25, 1998.

223 the red spoon: General Mills Public Relations material, "The Story of Betty Crocker," n.p., n.d.

223 "the red spoon is the more attractive": "Calling Betty Crocker," *Forbes,* August 1988.

223 red spoon graces more than 200 products: "Tale of Two Kitchens," *Atlanta Journal and Constitution,* June 24, 1999.

223 Norman Rockwell, painted their interpretations of America's First Lady of Food: General Mills, "Betty Crocker . . . 1921–1954"; General Mills internal document, "Betty Crocker portrait project," 1954, General Mills Archives.

   269

225 friend Muriel Wadsworth: PRIMETIME/*CapeCod Times,* "Model for an Icon," January 2001, p. 12.

225 "have never really personified Betty Crocker": General Mills, "Interview with Mercedese (sic) Bates," n.d., p. 1, General Mills Archives.

225 *McCall's* illustrator, Joe Bowler: Ibid.

229 "Elizabeth rather than Betty": Lee Egerstrom, "Corporate Betty Crocker Improves with Age," *St. Paul Pioneer Press,* October 28, 1980, p. 144.

229 Betty Crocker alive, vibrant, and attuned: General Mills Archives, General Mills internal memo to J. McFarland, October 10, 1968; letter to Joe Bowler from Joe Weaver, February 24, 1969, General Mills Archives.

229 "dead ringer for Mary Tyler Moore": Colin Covert, "Betty Crocker, at 65, looks like a million bucks," *Minneapolis Star Tribune,* May 23, 1986, pp. 1A, 9A.

232 In July 1972, the Minneapolis–St. Paul chapter of the National Organization of Women (NOW): Mary Hart, "Betty Crocker: A symbol of sexism, or of service?," *Minneapolis Star Tribune,* August 1, 1972; "NOW Files Bias Charge Against General Mills," July 26, 1972.

233 "Betty Crocker is just another advertising gimmick": Barbara Flanagan, "Cheers for Betty Crocker," *Minneapolis Star Tribune,* August 31, 1972.

233 Betty's 1972 portrait update was back on schedule: Series of General Mills 1972 internal memos between James Fish, Joe Weaver, Robert J. Blake, and D. W. Latterall, regarding the use of Betty Crocker's portrait, General Mills Archives.

235 New York artist Harriet Pertchik: Michelle Slatan, "Look It's Betty Crocker! She's New and Improved," *Newsday,* May 23, 1986, p. 1.

238 "a professional woman, approachable, friendly, competent and as comfortable in the boardroom as she is in the dining room": General Mills, "The Story of Betty Crocker," n.p., n.d.

238 Betty Crocker, at 65, Looks Like a Million Bucks": Colin Covert, 1986.

238 Betty Crocker had turned sixty-five yet never looked younger: Ibid.

238 National Public Radio newscaster Linda Wertheimer: "Betty Crocker Moving Front and Center Again," *All Things Considered*, September 11, 1995.

238 "The First Lady of Desserts": Betty Crocker dessert advertisement in Sunday paper circular, 1988.

239 *The Spirit of Betty Crocker:* General Mills Press Release, "Celebrating the Spirit of Betty Crocker on her 75th Anniversary," September 11, 1995.

239 The Betty Crocker 75th Anniversary Diamond Sweepstakes: "Iowan Wins .75 Carat Diamond Pendant in Betty Crocker 75th Anniversary Sweepstakes," *Business Wire*, July 3, 1996.

239 essay contest: "Celebrating the Spirit of Betty Crocker on her 75th Anniversary," September 11, 1995.

240 "Every age, occupation and walk of life is invited": Ibid.

240 210 television and 559 radio stations and 1,500: General Mills Press Release, "General Mills Announces 75 Winners of Betty Crocker Search," January 31, 1996.

240 "There's a little bit of Betty Crocker in everyone": "Celebrating the Spirit of Betty Crocker on her 75th Anniversary," September 11, 1995.

240 "will be less white bread and more whole-wheat": " 'Facing' Reality: New Image for Betty Crocker to Reflect Ethnic Diversity," *The Wall Street Journal*, September 12, 1995.

240 "we weren't allowed to see photos of the women": "General Mills

Announces 75 Winners of Betty Crocker Search," January 31, 1996.

240 "For me the phrase 'Spirit of Betty Crocker' conjures images": General Mills Public Relations material, "The Story of Betty Crocker," n.p., n.d.

241 "I'm happy to be a part of this history": Harry Levins, "Blending in Affton Woman's Face Becomes Part of Latest Betty Crocker," *St. Louis Post Dispatch*, February 1, 1996.

241 "I'm proud to be a part of her today": "General Mills Unveils the Betty Crocker 75th Anniversary Portrait," *Business Wire*, March 19, 1996.

241 Each of the seventy-five would receive a 1.3 percent representation: Harry Levins, "Yes, I'm There," *St. Louis Post-Dispatch*, March 20, 1996.

241–43 "Painting the portrait of Betty Crocker was a daunting task": "General Mills Unveils the Betty Crocker 75th Anniversary Portrait," *Business Wire*, March 19, 1996.

243 350 million media impressions in just one year: General Mills Public Relations recap video, 1996.

243 voiced a few mild quibbles: "So long, Betty," *Christian Science Monitor*, September 21, 1995.

244 Betty Crocker and her African-American counterpart, Aunt Jemima: Bill Maxwell, "Betty Reflects Ethnic Health," *St. Petersburg Times*, March 28, 1996.

244 Bob Crocker: Kathleen Parker, "New 'Betty' Forgot Male Gender," *Franklin* (PA) *News-Herald*, March 27, 1996; Suzanne Fields, "'A New' Betty Crocker," *Birmingham News*, September 1995; Kathleen Parker, "What Next: A She-Male Crocker?," *Reading* (PA) *Times*, April 8, 1996.

Acknowledgments

I wish to thank General Mills' archivist, Katie Dishman, for granting me access to the corporate archives, embracing my research, helping to separate fact from fiction, and for being a good friend. The staff at General Mills are wonderfully supportive and helpful, in particular Tom Forsythe. Thank you for the opportunity to explore Betty Crocker on her home turf. And a special thank you to Mary Bartz—once a Betty Crocker, always a Betty Crocker.

Finding Betty Crocker proved to be an incredible journey and I have David Wiggins to thank for believing in me and Denise Roy to thank for believing in this book. I am eternally grateful. I also wish to extend my gratitude to the talented team at Simon & Schuster for giving this book life, and to Dawn Frederick and Laurie Harper of the Sebastian Agency for cheering me on.

I received extraordinary help and guidance from Professors Elaine Tyler May, Sara Evans, Karal Ann Marling, and Peter Lock. I also gained wonderful insights from another Betty authority, Laura Shapiro.

Thanks to the following for aiding me in my research: the Minnesota Historical Society; John Rockwell of the Norman Rockwell Family Agency; Mary Anna Dusablon; Carrie Smith; Lynne

Olver, of Food Timeline; the Minneapolis Library Special Collections; the Hennepin History Museum; the Child family; and the Gale family, especially Jerry Gale.

Thank you to JoEllen Lundblad and Connie Hessburg from the University of Minnesota's Master of Liberal Studies Program, for your ongoing support. I am also grateful to Dave Stevens of the Mill City Museum.

I am deeply indebted to several former Betty Crocker staffers who were kind enough to share their "Crockette" stories: Thank you to Pat Anfinson, Mable Martin, Dee Young, Marian Ralston, Sally Swindler, Jeannette Ludcke, Bernie Peterson, Susan Peters, Emma Louise McClean, Karen Broughton, Lillian Anderson, Diane Deneke, Jane Hand, Marjie Fields, Ellen Sreenan, and the wonderful Marge Gibson. And a very special thank you to a true one-of-a-kind, Ruby Peterson.

I am so grateful to everyone who took the time to send me personal stories about Betty Crocker. Thank you for sharing your wonderful take on America's curious relationship with this advertising icon.

To the good people at Broad Daylight Productions, Target Media Center, and Blue Moon Productions, thank you for listening to me speak of Betty, day in and day out, year after year. (I promise to find a new topic!) Your input, kindness, and support are invaluable—thank you for being the best.

To my friends and family, thank you from the bottom of my tiny little heart for your unconditional support. And to my parents, Alice and Sam Marks, my grandmother Ruth Springer, and my dear friend Julie Ann Meyer, thank you for being there for me all these years. And to my husband, Robert, thank you for your love and for putting up with the "other woman" in our lives.

All photographs and illustrations courtesy
of the General Mills Archives.

Betty Crocker, Gold Medal Flour, Bisquick,
Wheaties, and Cheerios are registered trademarks
of General Mills, Inc.

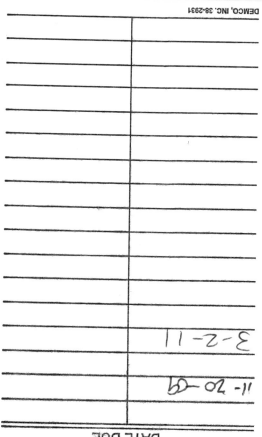

DATE DUE

3-2-11

11-20-09

DEMCO, INC. 38-2931